PRAISE FOR *THE SOUL OF SELLING*

"Carol helps people enjoy and succeed at selling. They tap into their own authentic passion and honor the people they talk to. They know they're acting with integrity, so they relax into getting their results with ease and grace. *The Soul of Selling* shows people how to be good, do well and have fun."

> — LEE GLICKSTEIN, founder of Speaking Circles International and author of *Be Heard Now: How to Speak Naturally and Powerfully in Front of Any Audience*

"Anyone who sells or works with people can use *The Soul of Selling's* six steps to get the results they want, and at the same time inspire trust, loyalty, and well-being. It's a joy to watch this material in Carol's hands. People soak up new skills, beam with enthusiasm and then go out there and get results they never thought possible."

> — TOM LENOBLE, Senior Customer Service Executive and Coach

"*The Soul of Selling* brings out the best in people, and gives new life to any sales force or business. Newcomers can win right out of the gate, and professionals can get renewed. People become the source of their own success, energized by their own values and so they get the results they want in a way that fulfills them and inspires others."

> — MURRAY THOMPSON, Ph.D., Consultant and strategist to *Fortune 100* companies

"I'm inspired! This approach gets people excited about selling and helps them do it in their own natural style. *The Soul of Selling* ignites that fusion of enthusiasm, personal power, and compassion that makes for happy people with great results."

> — SCOTT MONTGOMERY, Senior Vice-President, Geographic Expeditions, San Francisco

CAROL COSTELLO

How to Achieve
Extraordinary
Results with
Remarkable
Ease

THE
SOUL
OF
SELLING

(without losing your soul in the process)

BENBELLA

BENBELLA BOOKS
Dallas, Texas

BenBella Books
6440 N. Central Expressway, Suite 617
Dallas, TX 75206
www.benbellabooks.com
Send feedback to feedback@benbellabooks.com

PUBLISHER:	Glenn Yeffeth
EDITOR:	Shanna Caughey
ASSOCIATE EDITOR:	Leah Wilson
DIRECTOR OF MARKETING/PR:	Laura Watkins

Printed in the United States of America
10 9 8 7 6 5 4 3 2 1

Library of Congress Cataloging-in-Publication Data
Costello, Carol.
    The soul of selling : how to achieve extraordinary results with remarkable ease (without losing your soul in the process) / Carol Costello.
        p. cm.
    ISBN 1-932100-54-7
    1. Selling. I. Title.
HF5438.25.C6755 2005
658.85--dc22

2004019494

Cover design by Todd Bushman
Text design and composition by John Reinhardt Book Design

Distributed by Independent Publishers Group
To order call (800) 888-4741 • www.ipgbook.com

For special sales contact Laura Watkins at laura@benbellabooks.com

This book is dedicated to my Aunt Mary Ann,
who showed me the richness and joy
of connecting with people.

Contents

ACKNOWLEDGMENTS

Thank you to all this book's aunts and uncles—the thoughtful and generous people who have supported me in writing it, and in life.

FOREWORD

The most sought-after people in business today want more than just money and status. They want a greater sense of purpose and meaning in their work. They want to do well, but they also want to do *good*. They want to look in the mirror at the end of the day and know that they have made other people's lives better, that they have lived in alignment with their personal values and that they have fed their souls.

For people in sales, these needs show up in Technicolor. They *must* produce results, but very few are satisfied with doing *only* that. The old sales models don't always allow them to combine high results with personal values. Increasingly, they are turning away from anything that smacks of manipulation, pressure, or lack of respect. They want to be top producers, but they need a sales model that gives them great results *and* connection with personal meaning and purpose.

The Soul of Selling is this new paradigm. It offers a road map through the new landscape of high performance combined with "soul-fullness." It is a handbook for the new breed of selling stars. These people get powerful results, but they also follow their own moral compass. They bring their own values to selling, and create meaning in their work beyond the numbers they post. The six steps of the Soul of Selling method guarantee results, but they also guarantee that each potential client or customer is treated with respect and appreciation—whether or not they buy.

This method brings soul to the powerful, and power to the already "soul-full." People in large, performance-driven organizations get a way to bring forth their own natural integrity and authentic passion. People and organizations already focusing on values and contribution enhance their capacity to produce extraordinary results with honor and ease. The Soul of Selling works equally well for people involved in large corporate ventures, individual professional practices, community service campaigns or organizations, fundraising, multi-level marketing and any venture that asks people to get on board with a product, service, project or vision.

Carol Costello embodies this combination of high performance and personal values. She has put three companies on the map during her thirty-year career in sales, and developed the Soul of Selling method out of her own desire to produce powerful results, while at the same time sustaining and nurturing her soul. She has taught this approach for the last six years to groups that included top sellers, professional practitioners and soccer moms newly appointed to chair the bake sale. She knows what it means to take a stand for a result or cause, and to bring that vision into reality with integrity, passion and ease. And she has a track record for inspiring others to do the same.

The Soul of Selling can change your life. It can give you the power to bring your own vision to life and make it real, and it can show you how to get those results in a way that feeds your soul.

Murray Thompson, Ph.D., Consultant to Fortune 100 companies

INTRODUCTION

I began my sales career at an organization that lived and breathed big numbers. They wanted huge results, right now. They didn't care if you liked it, if you burned out, or if you operated with integrity. The numbers came first, at any cost. If you didn't deliver, you were toast. I was a sponge, and learned everything I could from them.

Then, driving to work one morning, a booming voice in my head asked, *Is life worth living this way?* The answer was *No*, and I gave notice that afternoon.

I left there exhausted and somewhat shaken, but with an inexplicable urge to keep selling. I had seen the power of it. I had seen what it was to have a big idea, and then bring that idea into reality so that it made an impact on the world. I had learned what it was like to *choose* your results, rather than to wait and see what happened. That was irresistible. But how to do it, and remain sane? How to do that, and be a good person? How to do that, and not only save my soul, but feed it?

I thought the answer was selling a different product. So I took what I'd learned at the "boot camp selling" company and joined another company that I believed would make a positive contribution to the world. It did, and I produced numbers that made it a successful global venture. But not without breaking a few arms and legs—the customers' and my own.

This taught me that it's not necessarily *what you sell* that feeds your soul, but *how you sell it*. I knew how to get great sales results. Now I wanted to combine those great results with honoring and contributing to the people to whom I sold, as well as with my own personal growth and well-being. Most people assured me that these three things—big results, honoring sales contacts, and feeding my soul—couldn't go together. You might get two of them, but you couldn't have all three. (The most likely combination was honoring contacts and feeding the soul,

1

but they assured me that I could forget about results with those two in play.)

But I knew it was possible to be extraordinarily successful in sales, and at the same time honor myself and other people. I didn't know exactly how that worked, but I knew the answer was out there somewhere.

Over the next several years, I was the first Director of Sales at two more start-ups that are still thriving today. In that time, I stepped into more potholes than you can imagine. My advantage was being willing to crawl out of each pothole, dust myself off, learn something and keep going. Gradually, with the help of hundreds of people, I developed a new way to sell. This new method yielded the same big numbers, but it also fed my soul. It gave selling meaning, purpose and inspiration. It gave me a way to thrive, as well as to succeed.

I call this method the Soul of Selling. It has been the making of me, and of many other people who wanted to feed their souls, contribute to others and make an impact on their world. They have used it to launch products, put their business on the map, work in communities and promote large visions like peace and human rights.

We all want the capacity to make our visions real, to make our projects fruitful and to make our products or services successful. When you can "sell" with soul, you can be profoundly effective, and at the same time enjoy and build your personal values, self-esteem and sense of fulfillment.

That is what I wish for you, and that is the purpose of this book. In the Soul of Selling seminar, I try to bring everything I've learned in thirty years—all the pothole-stepping, as well as the rich, melt-in-your-soul lessons—into one day. We make good progress, but this book gives you more time to digest the material and make it your own. That's how it's designed to work. Take what you like from here, make it your own, shape it to fit your situation and have a ball!

Carol Costello

P.S. Let me know how The Soul of Selling is working for you. Send your feedback to carol@soulofselling.com.

PART 1

Part 1 gives you an overview of the Soul of Selling approach, previews the six steps, provides a "well" of inspiration and shows you how to master the Discomfort Dilemma. The information and tools in these four chapters prepare you to make the six steps your own.

THE SOUL OF SELLING: HOW AND WHY IT WORKS

CHAPTER 1

The Magic Bullet:
Why the Soul of Selling Works–Every Time

What if you could guarantee the exact sales results you wanted, every time? What if you also knew that you were acting with integrity, that you were honoring and appreciating each person with whom you spoke—whether or not they bought? And what if, on top of that, you got genuine pleasure from selling, and even began to relax into doing it with ease?

The Soul of Selling offers you exactly that. You get extraordinary re-sults, and thrive because you are feeding your soul with personal values, higher purpose and a meaningful contribution.

You are being good, and doing well. This is the "magic bullet" every-one wants. You get people on board with your product, service, project or vision, while still growing into the person you've always wanted to be.

The Soul of Selling is a new paradigm for sales. It invites you to shift how you see "selling," to think of it not as pushing, manipulating, con-ning, or pressuring—but as a way of contributing to life and feeding your soul. You take a stand for something that you find valuable, and serve others by offering it to them in a respectful, honoring way. When you see selling as service, you are free to go all out. You can bring your-self 100% to the task, and that makes everything easier and more fun.

The six steps of the Soul of Selling guide you through this process, so that you sell with mastery, grace and the results of your choice. Your inspiration comes from within, from your own core values, and so you can renew it, reignite it, or realign it at will. You act with integrity, out of your own natural capacity to inspire. You can finally be yourself, get great results and feel good about how you get them.

You do not have to be a natural seller, or an experienced seller, to succeed with this method. Selling is an acquired skill. I am not a natural seller. I developed the Soul of Selling out of my own desire to make the things that I loved available to more people, and at the same time to succeed in the world, act with integrity and feed my soul. All you have to do to succeed with this method is follow the six steps. Whatever your dreams, your visions, or your goals, the Soul of Selling will help you step up to the plate and make them a reality.

THE FOURFOLD GUARANTEE

The Soul of Selling offers you a Fourfold Guarantee for **Results, Integ-rity, Passion** and **Ease**. When you can make that guarantee, selling is sweet. (And R-I-P-E!) You take the guesswork out of results, and the stress out of selling. Each time you begin a selling project, you know that you can guarantee:

1. *Results.* You get precisely the sales numbers you choose, every time.
2. *Integrity.* Everyone you contact is respected, appreciated and hon-ored—whether or not they buy. You can trust yourself never to con, bully, or otherwise manipulate your customers, your product or service, or yourself.
3. *Passion.* You find a new energy based on what you truly value. Your unique brand of enthusiasm comes to the surface, and makes selling fun.
4. *Ease.* You can relax. You don't have to second-guess yourself, your methods, or your motives. You can just follow the six steps, be yourself and enjoy both the process and the outcome.

The Fourfold Guarantee works for professional salespeople, entre-preneurs, first-time sellers, small business owners, bake sale chairs, fundraisers, multi-level marketers, community leaders, individuals with professional practices and anyone else who wants to inspire others to support their product, service, project, or vision.

WHY IS IT "THE SOUL OF SELLING"?

"Soul" is the part of us that craves higher purpose, authentic relationships and meaningful contribution. *Webster's* calls it "the seat of real life or vitality; the source of action; the animating or essential part; the moving spirit, the heart."

"Selling" is simply offering your product or vision in such a clear and inviting way that people see value in it for themselves and come on board. Selling might mean offering a computer or insurance plan in the marketplace. It might mean lining up people for a car wash on Saturday, or collecting money for the kids' baseball uniforms, or inviting people to join a book group. It might mean inspiring people to be part of a program to end hunger in the world, or to support world peace.

The Soul of Selling is based on three principles:

1. *We all want to have a positive impact on our world.* You might want to be the top software salesperson in your company, or help win an election, or spearhead an environmental cause. When you know how to "sell" these things in a way that gets results every time, you have the power to change your world.

2. *We all want to nourish our souls.* We want to be good people who act with integrity and contribute to others. We want to feel good about who we are and what we do.

3. *We don't have to choose between these two desires.* We can combine doing well and feeling good. Being a "go to" person who gets results does not mean you can't also be a good person who supports others. And being a good person does not mean you can't have a powerful impact on the world. In fact, a person of compassion, purpose and vision can do far more good if he or she also has the power to make things happen. A person who already has the power to make things happen will last longer and stay happier when he or she brings heart, soul and meaning to those results.

Our cultural and corporate values are shifting toward "soul." For those of us who sell, this means combining big results with self-esteem, higher purpose, growth, contribution and authentic personal values. It means finding a way to be successful, satisfied and congruent—a way to honor both ourselves and others, even as we put our product, service, or vision on the map.

The Soul of Selling gives the quest for the bottom line a moral compass, and shows us how to navigate the new landscape where results and values not only *can* meet, but also *must* meet.

The six steps are your handrails. They guide you down the path to becoming an amalgam of strength and contribution, of capacity and compassion, of steady will and generosity of spirit. They call forth your ability to produce extraordinary results, and to do so with meaning, integrity and ease. They foster genuine enthusiasm for sharing what you find valuable, and ask you to be the source of respectful, empowering relationships. They show you how to honor your core values, see your lessons, make gracious course corrections, take a stand for your visions and still get extraordinary sales results. You have the tools to be a force of nature—a force for good.

A SIMPLE, ELEGANT ANSWER

I grappled with how to sell *big* without selling *out* for twenty-five years, while acting as Director of Sales for three start-up companies that are still thriving today. I stepped into every pothole out there, climbed out, dusted myself off and figured out what I could have done to avoid the problem.

Finally, I had a map of where the potholes were. I found a way to sell exactly what I promised, and also to know in my bones that everyone I contacted was better off than they had been before we talked. I learned how to inspire myself, and how to keep that inspiration fresh and authentic. I could finally relax and enjoy some peace and ease in selling, as well as great results. I could take pride in what I did, and how I did it. I could enjoy the fruits of being a big seller, and at the same time let it shape me into the person I'd always wanted to be.

For a secretly shy person who wanted both to contribute and to succeed in the world, this was heaven. I saw that selling could be a high calling. It takes courage, grit and a spark that we want to share with others. People who sell deserve all the support and encouragement they can get. I wanted to be on their team.

I broke down what I was doing into the six steps of the Soul of Selling, and started telling people about it. Soon I was teaching a seminar on this approach for people ranging from top professionals who sold millions of dollars' worth of products or services a year, to people who had just taken charge of their first church garage sale. Experienced professionals and rank amateurs, corporate big shots and fledgling solo practitioners, people who sold products and those who sold services all reported the same outcomes:

1. Whatever their results had been, they got better. They sold more, in less time, with less effort.
2. They enjoyed selling more, and did it with more ease—avoiding burnout and turnover.
3. They took greater pride in what they did, because selling became service.
4. They had a technology that let them repeat their success, and kept them thriving.

WE'RE A SELLING SPECIES

Most of us sell every day of our lives—whether or not we know it, and whether or not we call our job "sales." We can't help ourselves. When we human beings find something that is fun or valuable, we can't keep our mouths shut. We want to share it with the world, or at least a few friends. We want to scoop people up and get them on board, whether it's asking them to "buy" into a:

▶ Widget
▶ Professional service
▶ Multi-million-dollar contract
▶ Friday night dinner party
▶ Insurance policy
▶ Worthy cause
▶ Class or seminar
▶ Better results on a customer service team
▶ Real estate consortium
▶ Local park cleanup

When you know how to make these invitations with grace and mastery, life is easier and more pleasant. When you also know how to get the results you want, life is more rewarding. It doesn't matter whether you're motivated by love, power, generosity, profit, altruism, or any combination of the above. It's great to be comfortable with offering people something you've found valuable—and confident that you can talk about it in such a clear and inviting way that they see a piece of it for themselves and get on board.

THE RUBBER AND THE ROAD

Life will always hand us opportunities to "sell." The only questions are:

1. Will we have fun, or get cranky?
2. Will we contribute, or waste energy complaining that selling is difficult and demeaning?
3. Will we succeed, or will we fail?

This is where the rubber hits the road. At some point, we have to bring the conversation around to results, to specific outcomes and numbers. How much did you actually make in commissions last year? Did you, or did you not, get the contract? How many new clients did you bring in last month, and is that enough to pay the bills? Are people coming to the dinner party, or will we be going out for fried chicken? Will we build the new church, or not? Will what you're selling in multi-level marketing allow you to quit your job, or do you need to sell more? Exactly how much more?

In my sales seminars, this is the point where everybody's stomach tightens up. Their eyes narrow, their faces freeze, and I can see the balloons forming above their heads: Sleazy! Manipulative! Why risk being rejected, or failing? Besides, pressuring people is wrong! That's why I don't get the numbers. Good people can't guarantee numbers, or they risk being bad people! Everyone knows that!

This is where the trouble starts—in the seminar, in sales, and in life.

WHAT GOES WRONG:
THAT QUEASY, UNEASY FEELING

In the seminar, I assure people that oxygen masks will be dropping from the ceiling. I tell them to secure their own mask first, and then help others. They laugh, but tentatively.

For many of us, professionals and novices alike, "selling" brings up nightmarish thoughts, or at least a subtle but pervasive dread. The only way around this is to tell the truth about it. Before we can proceed with the seminar, we first have to surface all the squirrelly little thoughts that people have about selling and those who do it, about themselves as sellers, about their product or service and about the people they will contact. Otherwise, they will take all these fearful thoughts and queasy feelings with them when they go out to sell.

I give them twenty minutes to write down all this negative mental chatter. Then they call out their answers, while my assistant writes everything down on a huge tablet in front of the room. Some fifty minutes and thirty pages later, we all sit exhausted, staring at the tablet. As my assistant slowly turns back the thirty pages, we see phrases like:

- ▶ Selling is a sleazy game, and only sleazy people play it.
- ▶ Who do they think they are? Don't they know they're taking food out of my children's mouths when they don't buy?
- ▶ People will know I'm a weasel, and just out for the money.
- ▶ I'm not really that good a therapist, and people will find out if I put myself out there.
- ▶ The vitamins I'm selling aren't as good as we say they are. How can I stand behind them?
- ▶ People are miserly jerks, so I'll have to trick them into buying something they don't really want, and then they'll hate me for it.
- ▶ I can't take rejection.
- ▶ I try to be nice but they must see how pissed off and confused I am, so sometimes I don't even ask them if they want to buy.
- ▶ I'll fail.
- ▶ I'll succeed.
- ▶ I'll feel like a fake, sound like a fake, and even if I'm not faking people will think I am.

Much of what winds up on the tablet isn't actually true, or even what people really think—but the suffering they experience is real. These queasy, uneasy thoughts and feelings are snaking around in their conscious or unconscious minds, creating havoc and misery. Oddly, there is very little difference between the thoughts of top salespeople and the thoughts of novices. The top producers have learned how to hide it better, to talk about it more obliquely and sometimes not to let it affect them as much, but I am always amazed at what they carry around with them.

The first question I ask is, "How much of this is actually true?" People's fears are real, but most of them admit that the chances of these fears actually materializing are minimal.

Then I ask, "Can you see why selling sometimes seems hard, and why you don't always get the results you want or feel great about doing it?" They nod grimly, but at some point as my assistant keeps turning back through those thirty pages of mind-numbing thoughts and fears, someone starts to snicker. The things that go on in our minds are so wild, so abundant, so in conflict with one another and sometimes so ridiculous that eventually hysteria overtakes us and we can't stop laughing.

After a break, we settle down and start to take apart what goes wrong. Why do we get so crazy around sales?

WICKED OR WIMPY?

The conventional wisdom is that there are two kinds of people in sales. One group gets great numbers, but will stop at nothing to get them. The other group have kind, generous spirits, but they may or may not get results—and so may or may not have jobs, businesses, and incomes.

Nobody wants to be part of either group, so we freeze. We become like deer in headlights, staring into the bright light of our fears. We don't want to *be*, or to *seem to be*, like sleazy used car salesmen. We don't want to impose on people, lose our dignity, or be rejected. We are willing to forego clients and commissions, and even give up on the dream of having our own businesses, rather than get into the sales game. Even seasoned professionals who have sold billions of dollars of goods or services have these concerns. They wonder if they can call up "the magic" again, and make it work just one more time.

THE "STOP" RESPONSE

Confronted with the choice between Wicked and Wimpy, many people simply stop. They get so hopelessly embroiled in worries that they refuse even to try selling, and take themselves out of the game completely. Others just stand immobile in the middle of the field. They don't pick up the phone. They close the file with the list of people to call, if they've even brought themselves to make the list. They withdraw into themselves, rather than risk that their fears may be true—even when they know logically that most of those fears are ridiculous.

Of course, people who freeze in this way fail anyway. They don't sell the widget, get the clients, raise the money, or do the seminar they've always dreamed of doing. They don't build their businesses, make their quotas, get their projects off the ground, or share their visions. They don't grow or widen their worlds, make their contribution, or fatten their pocketbooks.

Their product, service, or vision never sees the light of day, and all the people who might have benefited from it never even get a crack at it. They withhold from people the contribution they might have made, and miss out on financial success, relationships and experiences that could empower, expand and enhance their lives.

That's what happens when we succumb to the "Stop" Response. But some people can't stop. It's their job to sell. Others took on a commitment to produce a certain result, or for some other reason feel they need to keep going, whether they like it or not. They often fall prey to the "Stagger" Response.

THE "STAGGER" RESPONSE

These people stagger forward. They tell themselves and others that they are "out there selling," but they don't bring all of themselves to the task. They have one foot on the accelerator and one foot on the brake. They have trouble picking up the phone when there is *anything* else to do. They have very clean floors, alphabetized spice racks, defragmented hard drives, living rooms full of needlepointed pillows and garages full of sorted and organized nails, nuts and bolts—but they don't have many sales. They often feel frustrated, powerless, cranky and out of control.

They trudge on—but in agony. Agony isn't a good thing in the sales arena, and so they don't get terrific results. That makes them even more miserable. Unless they discover some way to combine power and peace of mind, they find themselves with some difficult choices. They can go Wicked, and feel awful about themselves. They can go Wimpy, and probably fail. Or they can keep staggering, and succumb to the stress of playing, and usually losing, a game in which they are only half engaged.

This is no way to live.

WHAT IF?

What if selling were no longer an exercise in avoidance, or in powering over the discomfort? What if, instead, it were a chance to be the person you've always wanted to be each day, and at the same time be a star and make fistfuls of money by offering people a product or service you value?

What if you were so clear about the value of your product, service, project, or vision that you loved talking about it, and spoke of it with confidence and joy? What if you could just focus your attention on contributing to the person with whom you were speaking in the moment, and stop worrying about yourself or your results?

The Soul of Selling gives you these things and more. You begin to enjoy picking up the phone to tell people about what you're offering. You start to think of yourself as the kind of person who can actually say, "I will have twenty people in my seminar this week," and know that, without fail, you will have twenty people. Or, "I will meet that $500,000 quota." Or, "I will have three new clients in the next two weeks."

What if you had fun with selling?

THIS BOOK IS FOR YOU IF . . .

When some people hear the word "selling," their blood runs more quickly. When others hear "selling," their blood runs cold. This book is for both groups. It is for everyone who sells, invites, or in any way wants to call people to their product, service, cause, event, project, or vision. Whether you are an experienced sales professional, or recently nominated to get volunteers for the neighborhood association, you can exponentially increase both your results and your enjoyment of the process.

This book is not about marketing. It won't tell you how to define or reach your audience. It won't tell you how to write the world's best flyer or get on *Oprah*. Nor is it about figuring out people's vulnerabilities so that you can box them into a corner, ask the perfect questions and either shame or dazzle them into buying what you're selling.

This book is about talking to people face-to-face, or phone-to-phone—and interacting with them in a respectful, empowering way that honors both them and you. It is about the Fourfold Guarantee for Results, Integrity, Passion and Ease. It is for people who want to take charge of their relationship with selling—and enjoy all the financial, social, emotional and even spiritual fruits that come from selling big and being good.

USING THIS BOOK

This book guides you step-by-step through personalizing the Soul of Selling approach for your specific situation. It is also a place you can come for inspiration and regeneration.

Part 1, *The Soul of Selling: How and Why It Works*, gives you an overview of the method, the six steps that make it so powerful, the benefits you'll receive from using it, and how to deal with the Discomfort Dilemma that is always present in sales.

Part 2, *Your Six Steps: Making the Soul of Selling Your Own*, is a detailed description of the six steps, with exercises to help you tailor each one to your particular situation and use it most effectively.

Part 3, *Taking Charge: Becoming the Source of Your Own Success*, contains chapters on creating your Personal Sales Vision, giving and getting support, letting selling shape you into the person you've always wanted to be and creating a Synergy Group of like-minded sellers.

I suggest you get a special notebook for the exercises in this book. You can make a few notes in the lines provided, but then expand your answers in your Soul of Selling notebook. The more you give to this process, the more powerfully it will work for you.

STEPPING OUT

Nobody succeeds in sales without becoming the source of their own success. This method is about getting the ball in your court, and then letting it rip.

Nothing works unless you embrace it wholeheartedly and give it a chance to succeed. Researchers are discovering this about diets. Fats, carbs, proteins. Everybody has a different idea about how to combine them in order to lose weight. It turns out that the type of diet doesn't make much difference. What matters is how well people follow whatever diet they choose.

I invite you to try this method for three months. If you use it rigorously, my guess is that you'll start to fall in love with selling, and with the results you're getting.

Most people don't believe that you can both sell big and be good until they see *how* it's done. That's the subject of Chapter 2.

How the Six Steps Work:
Passing the Hors d'Oeuvres Tray

How can you be a good, honorable, person of integrity who doesn't manipulate or con people in order to get sales—and still guarantee the exact results you want, no matter what? Where do you go for passion and inspiration? And how can all of this be easy?

Only a handful of people believe me when I promise in the seminar that they can guarantee great results at the same time that they guarantee integrity, passion and ease. They contend that you can be a respectful, honorable person one week, and then switch back to guaranteeing results the next week—but you can't do both at the same time. They say things like:

- I can get the result, but don't try to tell me I'm being good to these people. I'm kicking ass, and doing everything I was trained to do to close and win.
- I love people and they open up around me, but I'd die if I had to make a quota. It's unethical to pressure people. I may not be cut out for this, because I won't compromise my integrity.

They're not sure that passion and ease go together, either. When they hear "passion," they think "driven." I invite them to keep an open mind, and listen to the Parable of the Hors d'Oeuvres Tray. It's a good way to see *how* the six steps of the Soul of Selling work together to produce extraordinary results with remarkable ease.

THE SIX STEPS

As you read the Parable of the Hors d'Oeuvres Tray, keep in mind the six steps:

1. *Put down your baggage (and fix what you can)*. We all have negative attitudes, beliefs and fears that keep us from enjoying and succeeding at selling. This negative mental chatter tends to gather in four areas: selling in general, yourself as a seller, your product or service and your customers or contacts. Step #1 identifies the chatter and frees you from those chains.

2. *Pinpoint your passions* in selling, in yourself as a seller, in your product or service and in your contacts. When you know what has authentic personal value for you in each of these four areas, you feel more confident and speak more effectively about what you are offering. This step keeps your inspiration fresh and alive.

3. *Create your Speaking Bank*. These talking points include all the information and inspiration your contacts need in order to buy, arranged in clear, persuasive sound bites of various lengths. You know exactly what to say, and how to say it in a clear, inviting way.

4. *Promise your result*. This is a new kind of promise, one that supports you rather than threatens you. It's the truing mechanism that guides you through any difficulty and anchors your success.

5. *Conduct the Ten-Touchstone Honoring Sales Conversation*. The first three touchstones of this conversation ensure that you respect, honor and appreciate your contacts—whether or not they buy. You are then guided through opening, conducting and closing a powerful sales conversation. If this conversation isn't fun, and if both you and your contacts aren't in better shape after it than you were before it, then you're not doing it correctly.

6. *Keep going until you get the result*. You simply repeat this relaxed, respectful conversation until you get the number you promised in Step #4. You move toward the result you chose, inspired by your own values, until you win.

In this chapter, we'll describe each step briefly. Part 2 of this book takes you through each step in detail with examples, strategies and exercises to customize it for your particular situation. For now, we will take a broader view so that you can see how all the steps work *together*. Hence, the Parable of the Hors d'Oeuvres Tray.

PASSING THE HORS D'OEUVRES TRAY

The Soul of Selling method is like offering a tray of delicious hors d'oeuvres to people you like and admire, and then continuing to make honoring, respectful, appreciative offerings until the tray is empty.

Imagine that you are at a party for friends, and the hostess entrusts you with the honor of passing the hors d'oeuvres. She hands you a tray filled with sumptuous delicacies and asks, "How many hors d'oeuvres will you 'sell?'" She doesn't say "offer." She says "sell." By that she means, "How many hors d'oeuvres will you guarantee that guests take from the tray?" (You might imagine our hostess as a reincarnation of Yoda from *Star Wars*, saying, "Do, or not do. There is no try.")

Your first thought might be, *I can't guarantee the guests' behavior!* or *I don't want to force them on people!* or *What will they think of me?* Then you pull yourself together and remember the six steps of the Soul of Hors d'Oeuvres Passing.

First, you identify any negative thoughts or feelings you might have about what it's like to pass hors d'oeuvres, about the quality of these particular hors d'oeuvres, about your possible limitations as an hors d'oeuvres-passer, and about the guests and how they might react to you. After you see what these thoughts are, you use the techniques you have learned in this book to let them go and switch channels. You focus instead on the results you want and on the fun you will have producing them. (*Step #1: Put down your baggage [and fix what you can].*)

Second, you intentionally call forth and appreciate the value you see in passing hors d'oeuvres trays, in yourself as a passer, in the hors d'oeuvres themselves, and in the people to whom you will pass them. It might sound like this: You're helping out the hostess, connecting with everybody at the party, and offering them a delightful gift. You are a great person for doing this. You look terrific, you're performing a service, and you're going to do a good job. You glance down at the tray and spend a few minutes appreciating those plump little olives in cheesy puff pastry, the sumptuous mushroom caps stuffed with crabmeat, the sassy broiled shrimps, the sensuous runny brie with crispy crackers, and the naughty little pigs-in-blankets sizzling away in the middle of it all. The folks at this party are wonderful, and you are going to make their evening even better. (*Step #2: Pinpoint your passions.*)

Third, you create in your mind a bank of things you'll say about the hors d'oeuvres as you pass them. You want people to have all the information they need in order to make a good choice. "No, those are not *turkey* pigs-in-blankets, Marlene. They're the real thing." "Yes, Ed, the shrimp are broiled, and marinated in a Thai lemon sauce!" You consider some engaging ways to invite people into the experience. "Flaky cheese puff pastry, Angela, stuffed with imported olives?" "Runny double brie with rye and caraway crackers, John?" (*Step #3: Create your Speaking Bank.*)

Fourth, you decide what promise you want to make. How many hors d'oeuvres do you want to "sell"? Your promise should stretch you, but be doable. You're promising "no matter what," so you'll choose a number that you're willing to get even if you have to pass the tray around the room more times than you thought you might. You tell the hostess, "Two trays full," or "One tray full," or whatever you are willing to guarantee. (*Step #4: Promise your result.*)

Fifth, you conduct the Honoring Hors d'Oeuvres Passing Conversation. You step out into the party, head and tray held high. This conversation has ten touchstones, and the first three are about respecting, appreciating and honoring everyone you encounter—whether or not they take an hors d'oeuvre. Before you offer the tray to anyone, you remind yourself of what you are willing to appreciate in anybody you encounter. You might be willing to remember that, deep down, these people want to contribute to the world. Or that they are courageous to get dressed up and come to the party, or that they are being kind to one another. They don't have to earn your respect and appreciation. You call forth this regard, and hold it no matter what they do or say. You include yourself in this respect and appreciation. This is what you're thinking as you lower the tray and offer the first person an hors d'oeuvres.

You look Sally in the eye and give yourself the gift of a rich, authentic connection with her. When people realize they are being seen with respect and appreciation, they usually behave very well. You're likely to get a good response. You can't count on that, though. The pleasure for you is simply in the appreciation, and you are willing to continue it regardless of Sally's reaction.

Sally takes a shrimp with a grateful smile, and you're on to Don. He says, "No, thanks," but you don't take it personally. He may be allergic to some of these hors d'oeuvres, or on a diet, or just not hungry, or lactose-intolerant to brie. But your interaction with him is every bit as warm as it was with Sally. (*Step #5: Conduct the Ten-Touchstone Honoring Sales Conversation.*)

Sixth, you continue your journey around the room until you "sell" as many hors d'oeuvres as you promised. You may keep your promise in the first five minutes, or you may go all the way around the room without "selling" a single hors d'oeuvres. What then? You simply go around the room again, creating joy and enthusiasm, and making sure you honor everybody at least as much as you did the first time around. You may look for some new people coming into the room, or for people you missed the first time around, but you keep going until you "sell" your promised number of hors d'oeuvres. You continue to have warm, authentic interactions with as many wonderful people as it takes to do that. You're having fun whether you go around the room one time, or six. Or more. (*Step #6: Keep going until you get the result.*)

The Parable of the Hors d'Oeuvres Tray is one way to see how the steps work together. Let's take a closer look at the steps in the context of selling, and see how each one leads to the next.

STEP #1: PUT DOWN YOUR BAGGAGE (AND FIX WHAT YOU CAN).

We all have psychological baggage about selling, whether we've been selling for forty years or four hours. If we don't have it from our own personal experience, we get it from society. The myth of the sleazy used car salesman, with his plaid jacket and pencil mustache, is only the beginning. These negative thoughts, beliefs and fears can keep us from enjoying selling, and prevent us from doing it with skill, ease and grace.

Bill, a very successful business consultant, said, "I spent the first three years thinking I was a pushy jerk when I made sales calls, and gritting my teeth whenever I picked up the phone. I couldn't even keep my wife and kids' picture on my desk. I still have to take a deep breath sometimes before I make calls, and tell myself I'm okay."

That is no way to do business, so the first step of the Soul of Selling is to bring this old baggage out into the light and look at it clearly. You have to know what it is before you can let it go.

WHAT COLOR IS YOUR SUITCASE?

Everybody's baggage is different, and there is no accounting for why certain people have certain kinds of baggage. The important thing is to know what your baggage looks like so you can identify it, and claim it.

In Step #1, you begin by writing down all your negative thoughts, feelings, attitudes and fears in four areas:

> ▸ Selling in general
> ▸ Yourself as a seller
> ▸ Your product or service
> ▸ Your contacts

Here are some perennial favorites. Be on the lookout for your version of these thoughts and fears as they bounce down on to the baggage carousel:

Thoughts about selling in general

> ▸ It's all a fraud. Selling is for "slick" people.
> ▸ You have to pressure people, and I don't want to do that. Even if I did push them, they'd just push back.
> ▸ Selling is hard. And there's some mysterious key to it that I don't understand.
> ▸ It's immoral. Even if you win, you lose because you've sold your soul.

Thoughts about yourself as a seller

> ▸ I'm terrified, and I can't do it. I'll say the wrong thing, and do a bad job.
> ▸ They'll avoid me because I'm sliming them. I don't want to be a "user."
> ▸ I don't want to be humiliated, embarrassed, or rejected.
> ▸ I don't need the stress of being a slave to numbers.
> ▸ If I don't sell big, I'll be a bad person. If I do sell big, I'll be a bad person.

Thoughts about your product or service

> ▸ It's not that great. Why should I suffer for it?
> ▸ It's so great that I'll never be able to do justice to it.
> ▸ I have to hide parts of it, so I feel like a phony. It's all smoke and mirrors.
> ▸ I've fooled people so far, but if I put it out there I'll be open to more scrutiny.

Thoughts about your contacts

> ▸ They don't want what I'm offering. They'll hate me because I made them do it.
> ▸ It's like pulling teeth. They should come to *me*.

▶ Even if they buy, they're just patronizing me.

▶ I spend hours with them, and then they say "No." They're inconsiderate, rude, shiftless and lazy. Even when they say "Yes," they weasel out of it.

▶ I'm sick of hearing, "I don't have the time," or "I don't have the money."

I don't need to tell you that it's foolhardy to try selling with these kinds of thoughts and fears grinding away just below the surface—or *on* the surface. It's like driving with one foot on the accelerator and the other on the brake. At best, you'll get the results, but be miserable.

Mental chatter will cause you no end of trouble unless you learn to manage it. It is the primary reason that people are not already selling with great results, natural integrity, authentic passion and remarkable ease. We will meet mental chatter at every turn, so let's look now at what it is and how to deal with it.

THE MENTAL CHATTER USER MANUAL

User manuals help you take control. They tell you how things work, and how to troubleshoot problems. Let this Mental Chatter User Manual show you how to keep negative thoughts, feelings and beliefs from getting in your way.

Mental chatter works like this:

1. *It is the mind's job to generate thoughts, so mental chatter is here to stay.* No matter what you do, or how much you want to get rid of it, mental chatter will never go away. The mind simply will not stop generating thoughts. Some thoughts are positive, some are neutral, and some are negative. The good news is…

2. *You have choices.* You don't have to run blindly after every fear or objection that your mind tosses up. You can stand back, observe these negative thoughts, and instead give your attention and energy to thoughts that serve you.

3. *Mental chatter is mostly about avoiding pain.* If you write down all the negative mental chatter that passes through your mind over a fifteen-minute period (and you will be amazed at how much this is), you will see that most of it is fear-based. It is about defending and protecting you from imagined physical, mental, or psychological pain.

4. *Mental chatter hates change.* It doesn't want you to do anything differently from how you have done it before. After all, you've survived whatever has happened up to now. Any change is a risk. Mental chatter sees new ways of thinking and behaving simply as opportunities for pain, and as threats to survival. It doesn't want you to rock the boat, and will always argue for the status quo. Mental chatter is always loudest in the face of change.

5. *Mental chatter hates getting specific.* Getting specific is also a risk. If you never put anything on the line by saying, for instance, "I will have two new clients by the end of the week" you never fail. Failure is pain, and mental chatter will do anything to avoid pain.

6. *The old strategies don't work.* If you try to pretend mental chatter isn't there, it goes underground and festers—only to reappear at the most inopportune moments. If you try to beat it into submission, you just feed it energy. It gets bigger and stronger. If you try to banish it forever, you fail and get frustrated. Even the greatest spiritual and selling masters have mental chatter. They just know how to keep it in perspective, so that it doesn't get in their way.

7. *The key to mastering mental chatter is to develop a new relationship with it.* Since it isn't going anywhere, and neither are you, you need to find some neutral ground. You need a place where you can both exist without getting in one another's way.

Troubleshooting Strategies

These strategies are the foundation for a new relationship with mental chatter. You will find these general guidelines peppered throughout the book, as they apply to specific situations. Here is how to contain mental chatter, so that it doesn't cause trouble:

1. *Identify the chatter.* Write it down. Name it. Get it outside of yourself so that you can observe it. Don't let it run around loose inside your mind, where it can get its hands on the controls. When mental chatter is an object of observation, it is not *you*. It is no longer running the show. You can look at it, poke at it, and examine it. It can't push you around.

2. *Check to see if it's true.* Sometimes mental chatter has important warnings. "Stop! Don't walk into that street without checking both ways!" "Stop! That deal sounds too good to be true. Better have somebody check it." These warnings have an entirely different tone and energy from, "Listen, you're just asking for trouble if

you make a sales promise or pick up the phone." When you have mental chatter down on paper, it's easier to tell when you need to listen and when you don't.

3. *Recognize it for what it is—mental chatter, not reality.* Most of the time, mental chatter has little or nothing to do with what is actually happening. Even when it looks like it knows what it's talking about, mental chatter specializes in interpretations and opinions, rather than in objective analysis.

4. *Let it be, without giving it much attention.* Don't try to get rid of it or beat it into submission. Let it run around and around on its hamster wheel as long as it wants, but don't let it dictate what you do, or don't do. Recognize it, nod to it, and then look away.

5. *Switch channels to something more interesting.* Shift your attention to something positive—your results, the fun you will have getting them, even positive thoughts that have nothing to do with sales. This book will give you techniques and strategies for switching channels.

As you work your way through the six steps of the Soul of Selling, you will see these principles and strategies in action. You will have a chance to use variations on these themes at every turn, and become adept at managing mental chatter.

Freedom

Step #1 brings you freedom. You identify exactly what your mental chatter looks like, and learn powerful techniques for putting down that baggage. You look to see if there is anything you really do need to fix, and are guided through fixing it. Then you learn to switch channels and give your attention to more productive and empowering thoughts. Chapter 5 takes you step-by-step through this process.

Mastering mental chatter can transform not only the way you sell, but also the way you live your life.

STEP #2: PINPOINT YOUR PASSIONS.

This step brings forward your authentic passions, and helps you focus them for results. Where is the real juice for you? You're not looking for what someone told you, or what you think you *should* say. You're looking to your heart and soul for what you genuinely appreciate about selling, yourself as a seller, your product or service and your contacts.

Having cleared away the mental chatter in these four areas in Step #1, you mine each of them for gold. What do you want most in each area? Are you willing to have those things? What is the best thing that selling could be for you? What strengths and qualities do you bring to selling? What are your favorite things about the product or service you sell? (These may or may not be the benefits everyone tells you to stress.) What are you willing to honor in everyone you contact? Where else can you find passion in the process of selling?

Your answers may surprise you. Sherry was a shy, quiet woman who had gone back to work at forty-six selling food supplements. "I was shocked at what I saw in Step #2," she said. "I realized that the reason I was attracted to selling was that it had no ceiling. If I get it together, there's no limit to how good I can be or how much money I can make. That's not how I usually think of myself. It sounds so crass, but I get a smile on my face whenever I think about it." Sherry came out of the gate a winner, at the top of her multi-level marketing group.

Sam, who had been selling cars for twenty-one years, surprised himself as well. "I've done this forever, and thought I was just going through the motions. But in Step #2, I realized how much I love seeing people's faces when they get behind the wheel of that shiny new car. Most of them are about to pop. They smell the 'new car' smell, and you can see it on their faces. I get a kick out of that, almost like I was doing it myself."

Everybody's passions look different. Hal sells high-end travel packages. He has always been a little surprised by his success because he has a quiet, reasoned presence rather than the flashy demeanor often associated with people in sales. He realized when he did Step #2 that, "I like the way I sell. I'm quiet. It works for me and the people to whom I sell. It's great to appreciate something I'd always thought might be a liability."

Of course, the most important passion to identify and develop is the one you have for your contacts. What good are you willing to see in every person you encounter? What are some bottom line appreciations you can make? Remember, they don't have to earn this honor, respect and appreciation. You give it freely and unconditionally. Tom is a tractor salesman, and was surprised at his answer in this area. "I see everybody who comes in as a person who works hard for their family, and who creates things with their hands that they leave behind when they go. I can give them a tool that makes their job easier, and I like that."

The more clear you are about the personal values you see in selling, in yourself as a seller, in your product or service and in your contacts, the more effectively you present what you're offering—and the more fun you have doing it.

Here are some of the values people have discovered while doing Step #2:

Value of selling in general

▶ Selling is an opportunity to offer people something that makes my life better.

▶ It's a chance for me to grow personally.

▶ It's a way to make a lot of money and get the success I want.

Value of yourself as a seller

▶ I enjoy letting myself get excited about things, and sharing my enthusiasm with people.

▶ I know how to get results in life, and can use that skill to make a lot of money.

▶ I like helping people, and I have fun with it. People respond to that, and to me.

Value of your product or service

▶ My software is elegant. It helps people do things more easily.

▶ I am a great therapist, and therapy helps people sort out their lives so they can move forward.

▶ This capital campaign is going to get our congregation the church we need.

Value of your contacts

▶ I know that everybody I'll see today has dreams and aspirations, just as I do.

▶ I realize that everyone with whom I will speak today loves people and is loved.

▶ I know that everybody wants to contribute something to life, and we don't always get recognized for that. Today, I'm going to be the one who recognizes that in people.

Chapter 6 contains specific exercises to help you identify your own personal values in each of these four areas. Once you are clear about these values and passions, you are ready to proceed to Step #3.

STEP #3: CREATE YOUR SPEAKING BANK.

Your Speaking Bank is made up of talking points that contain all the information and inspiration your contacts need in order to buy—arranged in clear, cogent and persuasive sound bites of various lengths. It is a cornucopia of dynamic statements that you can draw on as you need them. It includes:

▶ A broad vision of what your product or service can do for people
▶ Vivid descriptions of its features and benefits
▶ An example of its value, as well as uses that are not obvious
▶ The cost
▶ Any other information people may need in order to buy

Chapter 7 leads you through putting together this information, and then breaking it down into "bite-size pieces" or sound bites. The end result is a presentation that leaves people wanting more.

When you've completed Step #3, you have set aside the negative chatter, identified your personal passions and worked this information into scintillating talking points, so that you're confident about what to say in any situation. Now, you're ready for the big time.

STEP #4: PROMISE YOUR RESULT.

Making promises is uncomfortable for many people. I invite you to take a deep breath, and remember two things:

1. The Soul of Selling promise is different from any promise you've made before. It is designed to serve you, rather than enslave you. It works *for* you, keeping you on track and guiding you to your results.
2. Without this kind of promise, you will get what you've always gotten before.

We say "promise" rather than "goal" because a goal is something you move *toward*, but which you may or may not reach. A promise is something you say you'll do, no matter what. The only questions are "when" and "how"—not "if." Chapters 8 and 10 show you how to keep your promises with ease.

STEP #5: CONDUCT THE TEN-TOUCHSTONE HONORING SALES CONVERSATION.

This conversation is the foundation of the Soul of Selling. It guides you through creating and maintaining an honoring relationship with your contacts, talking in an inspiring way about your product or service, hearing what they need to say before they buy and closing the sale in a way that makes both of you feel like winners.

At the end of this conversation, you both feel great. You know whether or not they're going to buy, and so do they. You've honored them, yourself, your product or service and the process of selling.

We will go over each of the ten touchstones in greater detail in Chapter 9. You'll see examples of how this conversation can be used in a variety of situations, and learn how to tailor it to your specific needs. For now, this overview will give you a sense of how it works. Here are the ten touchstones:

1. *See people's value.* You don't wait for people to prove their value to you; you define the specific valuable qualities that you are willing to see in them, regardless of what they say or do. These might include intelligence, vision, openness, diligence, or wanting to help people. As you talk with them, you call up these values intentionally and let them live in you.

2. *Make this value the foundation of your conversation, whether or not they buy.* This touchstone is about *maintaining* the respect, honor and appreciation you began in Touchstone #1. Even as they voice their concerns, and even if they say "No," you continue to appreciate them. If you catch yourself *not* relating to them with respect and honor, you stop and go back to doing so.

3. *Connect with the person.* Before you start talking, you create a connection with the other person. There are many ways to do this: genuine warmth, humor, some small thing you say, or even an appreciative silence. You know when you're connected with people, and when you're just talking to them. We all do. It's as if you are standing beside them with your arm around their shoulder, and the two of you are looking together at whether or not what you're offering is right for them.

4. *Share your vision.* This is where you use your Speaking Bank, weaving together your talking points and delivering them in a way that the other person can hear. This is not so much a speech as it is a conversation about the features and benefits of what you

are offering, conducted in the context of your relationship with them. It is delivered out of your passion, whether that is quiet or effusive, and all your attention is on the other person.

5. *Find out the value to them.* People need to know exactly what they want from what you are offering. They need to know, for instance, that they want to mow their yard in forty-five minutes instead of an hour using your mower. They need this information, and *so do you*—because this is where you return if the sale starts to fall apart. If they can't decide whether or not to buy, they can simply put this value on one side of the scale, and what it will cost them on the other.

6. *Invite them to participate.* At some point, you have to pop the question. You have to take the risk and say some form of, "Would you like to buy this?" Some sellers find this the most uncomfortable moment in the conversation, *but most buyers do not.* People expect to be asked whether or not they want to buy. In many cases, they're waiting for it, figuratively tapping their feet so the conversation can move forward. One reason sellers sometimes dread this moment is that they might hear "No." That's just part of selling. If the answer is "No," then you know where you are and can move on. The trick is not to take it personally. You may also hear "Yes."

7. *Hear their objections without getting hooked.* Asking the question usually brings up any objections that people may have. You'll hear all the reasons why they can't or shouldn't buy—even if they have every intention of buying! "Well, I'd love to buy this but I don't have the money." "I'd love to do that, but I just don't have the time." People often feel compelled to say they don't have the time or the money, even when both of you know they're going to buy. Sometimes it is their way of saying to you (and to themselves) that they aren't spendthrifts or time-wasters. Your job is to hear them out, and to honor what they say and that they need to say it—but not to get hooked and collude with them about their limitations

   You might talk with them about their objections, and together discover that they truly cannot afford what you're offering. Or maybe they can, if they look again. Or maybe they simply have to put what you're offering on one side of the scale, and the cost on the other, and see if it's worth it to them.

   Selling is a dance. Something made them want your product

or service. But oops, it costs something! It's not free! Or it requires that they invest some time. But they like it. "Yes." "No." Back and forth. It's a natural process. Don't you sometimes go through this same thing when you are deciding whether or not to buy something? Have compassion, and help them make a good choice.

8. *Take them back to the value.* After they've had a chance to air their objections, lead them gently back to what they would want from your product or service if they were to buy it. Chapter 9 contains some very gracious ways to do this, and shows you how to handle circumstances under which it's better to talk later.

9. *Close the sale.* In this part of the conversation, you come to "Yes" or "No." After the close, you both know whether or not they are going to buy. You will learn in Chapter 9 how to do this with ease and aplomb.

10. *Validate their choice, even if it's not to participate with you.* Let them know that you honor their choice, whatever it is. Stay in relationship with them, and let them walk away feeling better about themselves than they did before the conversation—regardless of what they choose. If they buy, let them know what the next step is or what your next contact will be.

You will learn to conduct this conversation so that it becomes second nature, and one of the joys of your life.

STEP #6: KEEP GOING UNTIL YOU GET THE RESULT.

Here is your power. This is what sets you apart, and makes you a person of your word. This is how you guarantee the result you promise, every time. It's easy to keep going because the Honoring Sales Conversation is something you can do all day long with ease, grace and fun—and Step #6 is simply a matter of repeating Step #5 until you get the result.

Donna, who sells insurance, told me, "I thought at first that Step #6 would make me nuts. But when I started using it, it actually removed a lot of stress. My stress was about always wondering whether or not I'd make my goal. I put a lot of energy into trying to figure out whether to keep going, or to pack it in. Or how *hard* to keep going, if I decided to keep going—or in what direction. The anxiety was unbelievable! Now I know that I'm going to keep going, and how to relight the fire. It's clear and clean. I work hard, but the stress is gone. I was blown away when I realized it was actually more relaxing to do it this way."

Chapter 10 is all about doing what you said you'd do with mastery, certainty and enjoyment. You will learn how to deal with the negative mental chatter, and what to do if everything seems to fall apart. You will get tools to release yourself from the quagmire if things get tough, and to keep from getting into the quagmire in the first place. You will learn to love this step, and to appreciate it as the key to real joy in selling.

THE ADVENTURE

The Soul of Selling is an adventure. You're doing something that is rarely done. You are a person of compassion, honor and integrity who also gets the result every time. In one sense, you're out on the edge. But in another sense, you are held safely and securely within the six steps. If you follow them precisely, they lead you systematically and inevitably to your result.

You prepare in Step #1 by unearthing and then shifting your attention away from the negativity of the past. In Step #2, you fill those spaces with positive regard and value, so that you are 100% behind yourself, your product or service, your contacts and selling in general. In Step #3, you create the Speaking Bank that helps you communicate in a clear and inspiring way about what you're offering. Then, in Step #4, you make the promise for a specific result. Step #5 leads you through the Honoring Sales Conversation, keeping you focused on respecting and appreciating your contacts, and on speaking in a way that serves them. With Step #6, you enter into your power as you keep going until you produce the result you promised.

Along the way, there are potholes, course corrections, fun and growth. You master any complaints and crankiness that pop up, and shape yourself into the person you've always wanted to be.

In the next chapter, we'll look at some of the rewards of the Soul of Selling, and give you an intriguing look at what they may cost you.

CHAPTER 3

What You Get
(And What It Costs)

The Soul of Selling gives you what everybody has always wanted from selling, but was afraid they couldn't get—the Fourfold Guarantee for Results, Integrity, Passion and Ease. But it asks something of you in return!

It asks that you give up some old, habitual ways of thinking and acting, and embrace some new ideas about what selling is, and what is possible for you.

THE LONE RANGER AND THE RUBBER BAND

There are reasons we don't just abandon our bad habits and live smoke-free, broccoli-filled, yoga-strengthened lives. Comfort Zones are comfortable. And our ways of thinking and acting are subject to the Rubber Band Dynamic: unless we keep them stretched into the new shape, and give them some support, they snap back into the old shape. Before we know it, those sneaky old ways have rubber banded back into position—no matter how well the new ways are working, or how great the financial or psychological rewards.

People sometimes experience the Rubber Band Dynamic about two weeks after the sales seminar. They call or email to talk about the great results they are getting—but they miss the energy of the group, especially if nobody around them is using this new paradigm when they get back to their organizations, small businesses, or private practices. There is nobody to give them high fives, nobody with whom to share information about potholes or tell stories that elicit, "Yeah, that happened to me, too!" Instead, the people around them are often stressing out, burning out and not producing the results they want. The Rubber Band starts to tug.

Maury, who sells printers, put it this way: "I'm in a whole different landscape with the Soul of Selling. I have to keep a map of the new ground in my pocket, and keep looking at it. If I just start wandering, I'll wind up back on the old streets, where I was before."

Janet, who sells life insurance, said, "I can't just put myself on automatic anymore. With this approach, I have to stay awake and be present to what's happening. Tell me again about the hors d'oeuvres tray?"

The Rubber Band is less likely to snap back when you have someone, or something, to help you keep it stretched into the new ways of thinking and acting—and to remind you how great that stretch feels. To shift the metaphor a bit, we all need a "well" where we can go to be renewed, reminded of the advantages of the Soul of Selling, and given a pep talk.

Let this chapter be that "well" for you. Use it as your launch pad for the Soul of Selling, and as a place to replenish and re-inspire yourself. Reread it to remember the unique benefits you get from this approach, and to be reminded of what you need to do to get those benefits.

THE OBVIOUS BENEFITS

Some of the Soul of Selling benefits are obvious:

1. *You sell more.* You develop the habit of keeping sales promises, and that alone dramatically improves your numbers. Beyond that, it's more attractive to keep going because the six steps ensure your integrity, you can renew your passion at will, and ease replaces angst.

2. *You make more money.* The money may come from commissions, promotions, or from attracting clients to your own business—or even from starting your own business. When you sell more, you usually make more money.

3. *Every interaction is a contribution.* The Honoring Sales Conversation guarantees that people are honored, respected and appreciated. When you've mastered this conversation, you have the means to make each interaction enjoyable, productive and of benefit to everyone with whom you speak.

4. *You sell with less effort and more fun.* The worst thing that can happen to you with the Soul of Selling is that you have an inspiring

conversation with someone who doesn't buy what you're offering. That is not the end of the world, because the next step is simply to have that same wonderful conversation with the next person. It may take one of these conversations to make the sale, or ten—but you stay engaged and gratified.

5. *You have greater stamina.* You have a good time, see clearly that you are serving people, and know you'll get your result. You're less likely to burn out or to "gray out," staggering forward without the energy to go 100%.

6. *You become a "go to" person.* You've mastered keeping your word. People can count on you, and you can count on yourself. This capacity spreads across every area of your life. You can take a stand for a vision, a cause, a particular outcome, and for yourself—and produce tangible results that make those visions real.

7. *You have a technology for repeating all of the above.* What surprised me at first, and what always surprises people in the seminar, is how quickly they realize these benefits. After a very short time—days or weeks—they simply become part of who you are. You don't even have to think about them; you just walk around with them in your pocket. When this starts happening, remember to stop and congratulate yourself for what you've accomplished.

These are just the obvious benefits. They affect the *externals* of your life: money, position, presence and the capacity to produce results. The subtler, *internal* advantages go deeper and are even more powerful.

GOING DEEPER: THE INNER ADVANTAGE

The inner advantages generate the outer advantages of the Soul of Selling. These inner advantages include:

1. *You've mastered something challenging.* The Soul of Selling isn't for sissies. It asks you to make the uncomfortable transition from talking about results to producing them. It asks that you be the source of the inspiration and value, both for yourself and for the people you contact. It asks for a high level of personal power and commitment, as well as compassion and service. When you've done that, you've accomplished something—and you know it. Ironically, selling becomes easier as you meet these challenges.

2. *You never again have to wonder if you will produce the result.* You will get those results every time, if you follow the steps.

3. *You never again have to wonder if you are conning or manipulating people.* You aren't. "I can't tell you what a relief it is to get rid of that whole idea that I was pressuring people," Paula said after two months of the Soul of Selling. "I didn't realize how worried I had been about that until I started doing it this way. I was always second-guessing myself, and wondered if what I was doing was ethical. Now I can relax."

4. *You're in the driver's seat.* You're no longer waiting to *find out* what you'll produce; you are *guaranteeing* it. You call the shots. You say how many sales you'll get, and you get them. You say that you will honor and serve people, and the Honoring Sales Conversation keeps you on track with that. You know how to keep negative thoughts or feelings from getting in your way, how to create passion, and how to speak effectively about what you're offering. The Soul of Selling is entirely a function of your own decisions, your own inspiration, and how willing you are to succeed.

5. *Your confidence soars.* You are winning and helping others win. You know that people are served and honored in your presence. To guarantee both results and service is no small thing. Your confidence breeds more results, which breeds more confidence—in sales and in life.

6. *You become a bigger person,* with a larger vision for succeeding and serving others. You are at the center of a magnificent game, and exhilarated by the process. You are leading a life of contribution, and winning.

Anyone who has been selling for more than ten minutes knows that external benefits like statistics and money are founded on internal benefits like these.

...AND SKILLS GALORE

As you use the Soul of Selling and reap these benefits, you naturally master some powerful skills. You learn to:

▶ *Let go of ideas, thoughts and feelings that have made sales seem difficult, stressful or unpleasant.* You identify the specific thoughts and feelings that have kept you stuck. Then you let them go and switch channels, focusing instead on your results and on the people you are serving.

▶ *Serve others in the most basic, important way possible,* by seeing them as valuable, honorable people whom you respect and appreciate.

▶ *Communicate with clarity and inspiration.* You know exactly what to say about your product or service, and say it with genuine, natural enthusiasm within a powerful connection. You interact with people in an authentic and inspiring way—even when they say "No."

▶ *Fuse power and compassion into a solid, unbeatable core* from which you operate. You are at once the "go to" person for results, and the person whose compassion and appreciation honor others, yourself, what you are selling and the process of selling itself.

These skills not only make you feel good and bring great sales results, they shape you into a person who can contribute more to life, and who enjoys life more fully.

WHAT IT COSTS YOU: THE 3 INVESTMENTS

What does all this cost? Well, you get what you pay for. To get good stuff, you need to make an investment. The Soul of Selling asks that you make three investments:

1. Be a grown-up.

When I say this in the seminar, the whole room dissolves into groans. "Oh NO!" people moan, holding their heads in their hands. "I was afraid of that!"

Clearly, being a grown-up is something we all know about, and many of us dread. But what does it really mean? Being a grown-up means going about life, or the Soul of Selling, with a minimum of muss and fuss, a minimum of drama, a minimum of teeth-gnashing. It means moving forward toward the result you want, whether or not the next step seems like fun at that moment.

Being a grown-up simply means recognizing the next thing to do, and doing it calmly, purposefully, and fully, with ease and appreciation. The next thing might be picking up the phone, picking up the phone again, or pulling yourself out of your glumness or discomfort to listen to somebody's objections just one more time, so that they feel heard.

Here are some examples of how grown-ups behave within the Soul of Selling:

▶ You feel cranky. You're sick of serving other people and would much rather that someone did something nice for *you*, for a change. You want to sulk, but instead you take a minute to sit down and create intentional respect and appreciation for the next person you're going to call. You pick up the phone, and the person on the other end of the line has the best moment of their day.

▶ You notice that you are playing Spider Solitaire on your computer while on the phone with a contact. He probably can't hear the mouse clicking, and you're listening *really well* despite having just won a game and watching the fireworks explode all over the screen. But you know you're not bringing yourself to the conversation 100%. And you know that, on some level, so does he. You close Spider Solitaire and focus on him as if he were the last person on earth.

▶ The person to whom you are talking is getting quieter and less responsive. Your mental chatter gets grumpy, then agitated. "What a jerk! Wake up and buy!" it yells. Instead of giving the reins of this conversation over to the chatter, you remember that you're the one in charge. You realize that the other person may be quiet because he feels pressured or overpowered, and you dial back your energy a little. The other person seems to wake up, and starts talking to you.

▶ You notice that the other person is doing all the talking, and you haven't said anything in several minutes. "What a jerk! Slow down, shut up, and buy!" your mental chatter shouts. But as a grown-up, you simply lean into the conversation gently and focus it on what he needs in order to make a good choice about your product or service.

▶ It's two days before your sales promise is due, and you aren't even close. You want to throw the phone at the wall, and then beat the pieces to pulp with a sledgehammer. You want to make a ritual fire of your call list and it's okay if the ritual fire, you know, accidentally spreads to your whole desk and maybe even to the whole office. But instead, the grown-up in you takes charge. You gently invite yourself to sit down and take a deep breath. You assess the situation and make some new choices about how to use your time. Luckily, you also have available all the energy you might otherwise have spent smashing phones and dealing with the fire department. You determine to make a fresh start. You begin at the beginning, with Step #1. You move systematically through the steps until you are calling again, reveling in the Honoring Sales Conversation, and starting to get some results.

▶ You have had it with selling—FOREVER—and are thumbing through the Yellow Pages looking for plumbing schools. You never again want to promise a result or talk to another jerk who is taking the food from your children's mouths, just because they are too stingy or lazy to buy. Suddenly, you realize that your mental chatter has ensnared you, and that it may not be working entirely to your benefit. You calm down and realize that mental chatter is mental chatter—not reality. You remember that you have the tools to step outside of it, so that it doesn't dictate your behavior. You sit down, open this book to Chapter 5, and start following the simple but powerful instructions for dealing with mental chatter.

Obstacles and mental chatter are natural elements of selling. Being a grown-up just means facing them with grace and maturity. They are inevitable, but they don't have to cost you your peace of mind, your sense of self, or your results!

2. Follow the six steps of the Soul of Selling precisely.

This seems obvious. But you may have noticed that, when you first read the six steps in the last chapter, a little voice in the back of your head was making notes:

▶ Okay, I can do that one.
▶ I don't have to do that one. It's silly, and why dig up negative thoughts?
▶ That one's for beginners. I'm beyond that.
▶ Yeah, right. Other people might be able to keep going, but I have other obligations.
▶ I could never do that. I'll say I will, but I can back out anytime I want.
▶ Who's watching? I can skate without doing that one. It won't make any difference.

You may be tempted to fudge on the steps, to do them "in your head" or skip them entirely because they're either beyond you, or beneath you—or you did them twenty years ago, or you don't think they'll work, or *something*.

The only way to guarantee the result is to do each step fully and precisely.

3. Be the source of your own enthusiasm and success.

The Soul of Selling also asks you to be the source of your own enthusiasm, and the source of your own success. Nobody has to jack you up, or keep you focused, in order for you to succeed. You don't let your moods determine whether or not you engage in the sales process, or whether or not you get results. And you don't wait for "inspiration to appear." That's like saying you can't produce results unless lightning happens to strike. Instead, you create the inspiration yourself, whenever you want or need it, by following the six steps.

I have gotten some of my best results at very difficult times in my life, when I've been truly down-and-out, or just out of sync or cranky. I didn't stuff the feelings. I let them be, but I didn't let them touch how I talked with people or determine whether or not I kept going. In fact, the process of being in service to people and knowing that I would get the result made me feel better. Engaging fully in the steps took my mind off my own problems. And when I *did* get the result, I *definitely* felt better.

It wasn't always like this. When I first considered the possibility that I would have to be the source of my own enthusiasm and success, it made me angry. It wasn't fair, and I didn't want to do it. But then nobody did it for me. I sat there and waited, and nobody showed up. The only way I had any power over my results was to step up, take charge, and be the boss—whether I was working for myself, or for someone else.

That was the greatest gift I ever gave myself. You simply cannot succeed in sales for long without being the source of your own success—and that goes double for the Soul of Selling.

THREE-INVESTMENT SYNERGY

When you start making these three investments in the Soul of Selling, you see how they all work together and synergize one another. The better you get at one, the better you get at all three—and the better you get at dealing with whatever life, or selling, dishes out.

Here is how it works: Jane was trying to get her multi-level jewelry business off the ground, and she did everything "right." She bought a garage full of product, she went to strategy meetings and she talked to her up-line frequently.

But she wasn't making calls. Family dramas constantly got in the way. Each time she promised herself she'd spend the whole morning calling, something happened. Her mother's car broke down, and she had to spend the day getting it fixed and driving her mother around. Or her daughter, Valerie, got sick at preschool and she had to bring her home.

Then she would spend the rest of the day in a tailspin about being a single mom, and how awful her ex-husband Wayne was, and how there was no child support that month. She'd call friends, who colluded with her, and that would be it on the day.

"It was terrible," she said, "but one day I realized that if I didn't take matters in hand, I'd never succeed with this business. I bit the bullet and stopped the drama. I went back to Step #1 and saw that I had a lot of baggage about Mom, Valerie and Wayne. I did the exercises and let it go. If Mom's car broke, I told her I'd take it in the next day but that I couldn't chauffeur her around. If Valerie got sick, I'd go get her and put her to bed—but instead of going into the tailspin about Wayne, I'd pick up the phone for my business.

"It was uncomfortable at first, but actually it was a bigger deal to me than it was to Mom or Valerie. They were fine with it. In a way, I was using the drama not to make those calls. My business would never be where it is today if I hadn't done that piece of 'growing up.'"

Jane didn't stop having family dramas. She had an aging mother and a small child. Her life was full of family dramas, but she acted like an adult, followed the six steps precisely and became the source of her own enthusiasm and success. She simply stopped trading in her dreams of a successful business to indulge herself in those dramas. She realized that life happens, and handled events as they came up, but she didn't use the drama as an excuse to avoid calling.

Ed was fifty-four when he became a grown-up in sales. He was selling advertising for a Chicago magazine and hated his boss. He spent a lot of time on the phone complaining to his wife, Betty, about the boss instead of selling. His numbers went down, and he became more and more miserable. At one point Betty said, "Look, either quit now or get off the phone with me and make some calls. Using me to vent and then not making calls isn't getting you anywhere!"

Ed was shocked, so shocked that he actually stepped back and looked at his situation objectively. He wondered what he would tell his son, Jimmy, if he were in the same situation. "I felt like a damned kid. A brat. I went back and let go of the baggage I was carrying around about my boss. I saw that Betty was right; it was time to put up or shut up. Complaining just wasted my energy. I might as well be selling, like Betty said, and at least making some money. So I did, and I got great numbers when I put my energy there. Just like the old days. Thanks, Betty."

Ed took steps to deal with his anger toward his boss, but in the meantime, he stopped letting that anger consume him. He didn't let it get in the way. He was too busy pursuing his current contacts and prospecting new ones. Sometimes he hardly noticed that the boss was in the office, especially when he was going over his commissions.

Jane and Ed could have failed, but they were willing to make the three investments in the Soul of Selling. They grew up, followed the steps precisely even when they didn't want to do so, and became the source of their own success.

THE POWER TO CHOOSE

The three investments give you dominion in your own life. They give you the power to choose what to do, and then to do it. When you are willing to make these investments, you can use the Soul of Selling to get exactly the results you want.

Just as your contacts need to know the benefits and costs in order to make a good decision about buying, you need to know the specific benefits and costs in order to go forward with the Soul of Selling. To zero in on exactly what benefits you want to get out of using this method, and to assess what your own personal cost may be, do these exercises.

EXERCISES

EXERCISE #1: What are the specific benefits you would like to derive from using the Soul of Selling?

EXERCISE #2: Aside from the three investments mentioned in this chapter, what else do you anticipate your personal "investment" or cost will be when you start using the Soul of Selling?

▶ What, if anything, will you need to change?

▶ What is your mental chatter likely to sound like?

▶ What are your fears?

▶ What will it "cost" you to move beyond the chatter and fears?

EXERCISE #3: As you anticipate what your personal "cost" will be, what can you do to ease the situation, or to manage your mental chatter or fears as Jane and Ed did? For each item in Exercise #2, list the antidote or what you can do to manage that fear or negative thought.

CHAPTER 4

The Discomfort Dilemma:
Why We Want to Stop, and How to Keep Going with Ease

"There's a split second that defines each day for me," Jack said. "It's that instant when I'm deciding whether to pick up the phone and sell—or to play a computer game."

"Why do you want to play the computer game?" I asked him.

"Because the idea of making the calls is uncomfortable. When I'm actually making calls, I get into it. But the idea of them, before I start, just seems overwhelming. I want to do anything else. I feel like I need a break, even if it's nine o'clock in the morning."

"Why not go all out? Take the morning off, or go get coffee and a Danish?"

"Because I'm working," he answered. Then he said sheepishly, "Except, I'm not."

"Do you enjoy playing computer games?"

"Yes and no. It's fun. I numb out for a few minutes, but after a minute or two, I start feeling stressed and guilty."

"Why?"

Jack thought a moment. "I'm not doing what I'm supposed to be doing, and I know the calls aren't going to go away. I'll still have to do them, but I'll be behind. It doesn't make any sense. In the end, it's worse to play the game, but sometimes I can't help myself."

Jack is describing the Discomfort Dilemma. It happens in every aspect of life, but it shows up on steroids when you sell. People who love selling have almost always mastered the Discomfort Dilemma. People who do *not* enjoy selling almost always have *not* mastered it. You can succeed in sales without a command of the Discomfort Dilemma—but that's doing it the hard way, and it's not always a pretty sight.

The Soul of Selling asks that you do things the easy way. Your Discomfort Dilemmas may be light or intense—but you'll be ahead of the game if you understand what they are, where they come from, how they work and how to pass through them with ease and grace.

WHAT IS THE DISCOMFORT DILEMMA?

The Discomfort Dilemma is that perilous moment when you stand poised between moving forward and doing whatever is the next step in the selling process—or doing something to avoid it. That next step might be:

▶ Picking up the phone
▶ Picking up the phone again to make the next call
▶ Calling back the person you agreed to call next week (now this week) and who you're afraid will say "No"
▶ Making a cold call
▶ Making a promise for results
▶ Closing the sale
▶ Calling someone you consider intimidating, but who might be a good source of leads
▶ Anything that involves discomfort, the possibility of failure, or any potential for rejection—or that you just plain *don't wanna* do!

When you're on the horns of the Discomfort Dilemma, the next step always seems agonizing or impossible. You want to dive under the bed and mainline chocolate, or at least defrag the hard drive. You'll do almost anything to avoid the imagined discomfort of that next step—even when you know from bitter experience that trying to avoid it only makes you *more* uncomfortable. That next step is still before you when you finish mainlining the chocolate, but now it seems even bigger. It's later in the game. You feel even more behind the Eight Ball, and you're not sure you can trust yourself now. You feel as if, in order to make up for having gotten off track, you have to produce *more* results, *better* results, and you have to produce them more *quickly*.

GIMME A BREAK!

In the midst of the Discomfort Dilemma, almost anywhere seems better than where you are. And there are so many more comfortable things to do! You could call a friend. You need to keep up these relationships, after all. You could play with the cat. The poor thing needs exercise. And you promised Mark you'd show him how to back up his hard drive. You could email your aunt, or even pay the bills. Righteous activities!

Hey, you could shampoo the rug! Sure, it's "call time," but just last week you read an article on how crucial it is to shampoo your rugs on a regular basis to keep them mold-free and extend their life! Come to think of it, you read that article during a "call time," too. Which only shows how important it is to be flexible about what you do in "call time!" Otherwise, you wouldn't know about the importance of regular rug care—and you might be tempted to make sales calls, rather than doing what you *really* need to do, which is obviously to shampoo the rug.

Bills need to be paid. Rugs need to be shampooed. *But not during the time when you said you'd make calls.* During that time, cleaning the bird cage or fish tank are going to seem like good ideas—to say nothing of kicking back with a cup of coffee to chat with a friend, or surf the web for the perfect PDA.

Knowing that the Discomfort Dilemma will never go away, and understanding how it works, gives you a leg up.

WHERE DOES IT COME FROM?

The Discomfort Dilemma pops up when you start moving forward, or doing anything new. These things represent *change*—however small, and however good. Even if you're just making the same kind of calls you made yesterday, you are talking to new people and moving closer to your promise. That's change.

When change of any kind is in the air, mental chatter gets startled and wakes up—on the wrong side of the bed. It scowls and stamps. It pouts, and begins its siren songs:

▶ I'm only thinking of you. You need a rest. Take a load off. Relax! You'll do better in the long run.

▶ It'll sharpen your wits to play computer games. You need that.

▶ C'mon, don't be such a stick-in-the-mud! You're human. Life's too short to work that hard. Give yourself a break. Here, try this tiny piece of chocolate...

And before you know it, you're mainlining.

When mental chatter starts cajoling and nattering, remember that it does not always have your best interests at heart. You can postpone or delay whatever is next, but ultimately you have to do it. The longer you put it off, the longer you prolong the agony and the more uncomfortable it becomes.

WHAT YOU NEED TO SUCCEED

I struggled with the Discomfort Dilemma for years, and became a champion computer game player in the process. I also became quite anxious. The stress of backing away from uncomfortable "next steps," and then running back to fix everything at the last minute, double speed, started to take its toll. Cortisol and other stress hormones surged into my system until, finally, I reached my pain threshold.

I needed a plan to master the Discomfort Dilemma, and put together two sets of tools: one to prepare me to deal effectively with the Discomfort Dilemma, and the other to use when the Dilemma was already upon me. The rest of this chapter is about those tools. You can start using them today, and the Discomfort Dilemma need never stop you again.

BEFORE THE DILEMMA STRIKES...

In the world of selling, Surprises 'R' Us. We'll always have to think and speak on our feet, so it behooves us to prepare for anything we *know* is coming our way. The Discomfort Dilemma is one of those things. These three tools will help you get ready to handle the Dilemma with ease and grace.

1. Identify your "most likely" Discomfort Dilemmas.

We all have different triggers. What makes me crazy may not bother you. My biggest discomfort point might be calling people back. Yours might be closing the sale. When you know where your personal Dilemmas are most likely to occur, you have an advantage. They lose the element of surprise, and you are in better shape to handle them.

Where are your Discomfort Dilemmas? Do you hate that first call, but then pick up steam as you go forward? Do you want to stop after the first "No?" What about the first time you meet a contact in person? For many people, the Discomfort Dilemma falls right before they close the sale. They're willing to do everything until it is time to, as they imagine it, "put the other person on the spot."

2. Anticipate your "most likely mental chatter."

Each time a Dilemma occurs, it carries with it surround-sound mental chatter. And not just any mental chatter. The chatter you hear will be put together especially for you. It will consist of the specific complaints, arguments and whining to which you are most susceptible.

Mental chatter is no fool. It's not going to tempt you with grousing and whimpering that would appeal to somebody else. It will choose exactly the words that are most likely to make *you* bite! It knows where you are vulnerable, and zeros in on that precise spot. How does it know? It's been living with you for as many years as you have been alive. If subtle logic works, that's what mental chatter will use. If smart and sassy works, you'll hear that. If kicking and screaming draws you in, expect that. It might sound like this:

▶ Hey, you guaranteed you would do this with integrity. Shouldn't you balance your checkbook rather than make calls?

▶ Nobody's the boss of me. I know what I'm doing, and I say I need a break.

▶ It's just not fair. Other people don't have to be this uncomfortable.

Take the time to anticipate not only when the Dilemma will strike, but what it will sound like. Then you'll hear a piece of mental chatter float through your mind, and think, "Hey, that's exactly what was on my list of 'Most likely mental chatter!' It's floating through my mind, right now, as we speak!" The minute you recognize that, you are observing the chatter, rather than letting it drag you forward automatically. When you are observing something, you are slightly removed from it. It's not you; it's outside you and you are looking at it. It loses its power over you.

3. Find your "fixes."

For each of your "most likely" Discomfort Dilemmas, you need to devise a "fix" that gets you moving past that paralyzing moment of indecision and takes you into action. Laurie hated to make the first call of the day. She realized that she was uncomfortable switching from the personal activities of her morning—getting the kids off to school, meditating, stretching, and having a cup of coffee with the paper—to the activities of her sales job. Her "fix" was to spend a moment before she picked up the phone remembering a recent call that had been particularly pleasant, or even mocking up in her mind how she wanted the first few calls to go. That got her energized, and on her way.

Pete hated to call when he was behind schedule with his results. If his promise for Friday was fifteen sales and he only had four by Wednesday morning, he wanted to get on a plane to Tahiti—but he'd settle for Des Moines. Anywhere would do. He found himself "having" to go out to coffee with people, or spend time on the phone with his kids. He found that personal crises often tended to occur in these moments. And if nothing external happened, he would hear himself say, "Man, I have to clean up this list of prospects."

When Pete took the seminar and heard other people talk about their version of the Discomfort Dilemma, he had a moment of truth. He realized that the Dilemma occurred for everyone, and that he wasn't weird or bad because he got sucked into it occasionally. This somehow gave him permission to put in a "fix."

"Seeing that other people had the same thing made it alright. If it was okay to have it, it was okay to fix it! For me, that was half the battle. My 'fix' was dividing up what I had left to produce into the number of days I had to do it, and setting smaller interim promises for each day. If I had eleven sales to make in three days, that was four on Wednesday, four on Thursday and three on Friday. Looking at it that way shifted my perspective. I was going for four, not eleven, so I could get on it. Once I realized it was normal to have the Dilemma and that all I had to do was find a 'fix,' it was pretty easy."

Susan had just the opposite Dilemma. When things were going well and she was ahead of the game, she felt an irresistible desire to shop. Getting close to keeping her sales promise actually triggered discomfort. If her promise was to sell three houses in July and she'd sold two by the tenth, her office buddies knew they could find her at Macy's. But toward the end of the month, she often got crunched up and was desperate for that one last sale.

"My 'fix' really worked," she said. "When I felt that Dilemma coming on me and started to think about a suit I'd seen, I'd say to myself, *Just finish up your promise. When you've made it, you can spend the whole rest of the month in the stores if you want.*" She tricked herself into staying with it by promising herself rewards. And the rewards weren't just more shopping. She planned trips to Yosemite, the ocean, a Shakespeare festival, and Hawaii. This strategy kept her time filled with either: 1) Making good on her promise, or 2) Enjoying her reward.

4. Plan rewards.

Do what Susan did. Plan rewards for yourself. You might even create a bank of rewards where you can go in an emergency. When the Discomfort Dilemma is upon you, your mind won't want to consider ways to reward yourself when you finish the task. It will want to keep pestering you about not doing the next step. If your rewards bank is ready and at hand, you can simply reach there. You can pull out the list and see:

▶ Massage
▶ Walk in the park
▶ See a movie with the kids

Just pick something from the list, and promise it to yourself as a reward when you finish. Your reward can be anything from a gold star, to lunch with a friend, to a piece of jewelry—depending on the magnitude of the task and what you can afford. Be imaginative. One woman got a tube of thick, brightly colored glitter glue and saved it for Discomfort Dilemmas. When she completed the task she had been resisting, she ran a line of glue over it on her "to do" list. That may sound strange, but when it comes to the Discomfort Dilemma, you want whatever gets you through the night. That woman made more than $350,000 last year and I, for one, do not laugh at her glitter glue.

The better prepared you are to meet the Discomfort Dilemma, the easier it will be to walk forward without "postponing" or "delaying."

INCOMING!! TOOLS FOR MANAGING THE MOMENT

You've prepared for the Discomfort Dilemma—but knowing when your Dilemmas are most likely to occur, what mental chatter is likely to say, and what "fixes" you will use won't make you impervious. How do you manage the moment when you're standing in the midst of the Dilemma? The negative chatter is getting louder and more persuasive. You're starting to lose ground, and need traction quickly. What do you do?

Here are some tools you can grab quickly, in the midst of the Dilemma, to get back on track:

Tool #1: Define the task.

When the Discomfort Dilemma takes hold, it's easy to confuse one call with twenty calls, and with the follow-ups to all those calls, and with all the other things you need to do that day like grocery shopping, a staff meeting, a report and your kid's birthday party. Instead of one phone call, you're looking at a huge miasma of "to do's." It's staggering, and overwhelming. One task has become, in your mind, a shapeless and growing blob. There is no good place to begin, and it seems endless. You can't possibly face it, and that's why you have to retreat. The Discomfort Dilemma starts to pull ahead of you.

The first antidote is to define clearly the one task that is actually before you. Is it one call? Polishing one part of your presentation? Write it down, and be very specific. Only let yourself write down that one task.

If the one task involves several "to do's," list them. Define each one specifically. For instance, if the task is "Finish the sales report," your sub-tasks might be:

▶ Gather Bob's information.
▶ Gather Sally's information.
▶ Gather Gail's information.
▶ Make a chart.
▶ Enter the data.
▶ Write an interpretation of the data.
▶ Email it to Tom.

"Finish the sales report" can be intimidating. You know there are sub-tasks, but if you're not exactly sure what they are, they can quickly grow into the miasmic blob. Writing them down gives them definition and limits. You can just march down the list.

I had a mentor who likened this process to starting out with a colander full of spaghetti. All the strands were tangled up with one another, and you didn't know exactly what you had in the colander. You couldn't tell where one strand ended and the next one began. Defining the task before you is like taking all the pieces of spaghetti out of the colander, one by one, and lining them up next to one another on the counter. It shows you exactly what is there, and leaves nothing to the imagination.

Tool #2: Write down the chatter, and then turn it around.

When you feel yourself succumbing to mental chatter's siren call, take five minutes to write down everything it is saying. Again, putting these negative or fearful thoughts on paper, or in a computer file, places you in the observational position. You can *observe* them, rather than *being* them. Then take another five minutes to write down an alternative scenario or perspective on your situation. It might sound like this:

Mental Chatter: "I can't believe this class is only a week away and I still have to get twenty people for it. I bet there aren't twenty people in the whole world who want to come, and half of them probably live thousands of miles away. How am I supposed to pull people out of thin air, especially with that rotten promo material they gave me? And what about Sally? Where are *her* twenty people? She just spent a half hour talking to her son on the phone. She doesn't seem upset about not having her places filled. Some people have no moral fiber. And I feel awful today. That shrimp last night didn't agree with me. I'm pretty sure I have food poisoning. I should probably go to the emergency room and get it checked out. Then when they ask about the numbers, I can say I had a medical emergency. I was never meant to do this, anyway. What was I thinking when I said I would? Where's that emergency room number?"

Alternative Perspective: "The class is a week away and I still have to get twenty people. That business about there not being twenty people on earth who want to do it sounds a little extreme. I bet there are twenty people within a block of where I'm sitting who'd love to do the class. I just have to find them. I didn't like the promo material, but that's just my taste. Other people like it. Anyway, that's not my job. My job is to find the people and tell them about the class. What I do and what Sally does are apples and oranges. I'm comparing her outsides with my insides, and it's none of my business. I need to pay attention to what's on my plate, not what's on hers. I have a little stomach upset. I'll take something, and check it again in an hour. Meanwhile, I'll work on getting those twenty people."

Creating even one alternative to mental chatter's nightmare scenario defuses the situation. It can even make mental chatter's version a source of amusement.

Tool #3: Connect with your purpose.

It's easier to get where you're going if you know *why* you are going there. Tool #1 above tells you where you're going. You are going toward the next call, the report, creating the prospect list, or whatever task prompted the Discomfort Dilemma. Tool #2 removes some of the obstacles. Tool #3 tells you *why* you are going there.

Why is this particular task important? Your reason might be altruistic—to share your widget or vision with the world. It might be practical—to make money to pay the rent, or buy a car, or take the family on a great vacation. It might be all of these things. The purpose itself isn't as important as the fact that you *have* one, and that you know what it is. That gives you the energy to get there.

Tool #4: Be gentle with yourself.

In the midst of the Discomfort Dilemma, we have a tendency to be harsh and punitive with ourselves. We want to be "disciplined." We tell ourselves sternly, "Don't you *dare* start mainlining that chocolate! Don't you *dare* open that computer game!" This strategy almost always fails, and often produces exactly the opposite of the intended result. I have seen it turn fifty-year-old master sellers into recalcitrant teenagers who spit back, "Oh, YEAH!? Watch me!" Do what is there to be done, then let yourself relax into a feeling of accomplishment.

Mastering the Discomfort Dilemma makes you senior to any situation. You own the paradox of becoming more comfortable by doing the uncomfortable thing. That is a key to the Soul of Selling—and to a happy and successful life.

EXERCISES

Prepare yourself for your next encounter with the Discomfort Dilemma with these exercises:

EXERCISE #1: Make a list of your five "most likely" Discomfort Dilemmas.

EXERCISE #2: For each of these Dilemmas, make a list of the conversations your mental chatter is most likely to have with you.

EXERCISE #3: For each of these Dilemmas, find a "fix."

Part 2 takes you through each of the six steps in detail. You see how each step works, and personalize it for your own specific situation.

YOUR SIX STEPS: MAKING THE SOUL OF SELLING YOUR OWN

CHAPTER 5

Step #1:
Put Down Your Baggage
(And Fix What You Can)

In the next six chapters, you will customize each of the six steps so that it works best for you.

With Step #1, you leave behind all the attitudes, viewpoints, or concerns that have kept you from fully enjoying or succeeding at sales. You learn where this negative baggage comes from, what it does, and how to defuse it so that you can start anew with fresh attitudes and motivations that support your success.

PUT DOWN *WHAT?*

"Put down your baggage" simply means releasing any psychological baggage that could get in the way of your feeling good about selling, or prevent you from selling successfully. This baggage is made up of negative mental chatter that has congealed into opinions, beliefs, complaints, confusions, attitudes, decisions, worries and fears about selling.

Some common pieces of selling baggage are:

▶ Selling is extremely difficult. You have to kill yourself even to engage it, and you may or may not get the result.
▶ Selling is chancy business, a real crapshoot.
▶ I was made for better things, and I'm not happy about having to sell.

▶ I just don't have the hard core that it takes to sell.

▶ People are too cheap to buy this high-end service.

▶ With the economy like this, nobody's going to do well.

Oddly, it is not unusual for one person to hold all of these conflicting attitudes and beliefs. Baggage defies reason.

Do we really believe these things? Usually not, when we take the time to examine them. The problem is that we don't always take that time. So these thoughts and fears start slipping and sliding around in our brains, disguised as the truth. They become part of the background noise in our minds, and start to affect how we operate. We approach selling from the foundation of this baggage, rather than from our authentic desires and values.

When we actually examine what we have in our bags, most of it disappears. But first we have to open the bag, and that's what Step #1 is about.

HOW HEAVY IS YOUR PACK?

People new to selling usually approach Step #1 with relief. They are painfully aware of the negative thoughts, feelings and attitudes they have about selling, and can't wait to get rid of them. Veteran sellers are sometimes more skeptical. They are less eager to rock the boat, to unearth negative thinking that may be so far underground by now that they hardly even notice it. They are rarely encouraged by their companies to unearth this baggage unless it's affecting their numbers or getting in somebody else's way. The problem is that it's still there, whether or not they notice it. I am amazed at the amount of baggage that many successful people carry around with them, and often wonder what terrific results they would produce if they just put it down.

Several years ago, I hiked down and up the Grand Canyon carrying a forty-four-pound pack on my back. There are those who don't think a one-day stay at the bottom of the Canyon warrants forty-four pounds of gear, and still others who don't believe a hairdryer is an essential component of that gear. Be that as it may, we encountered along the trail several park employees who worked at the bottom of the Canyon for two- or three-day stretches, and who hiked to work with no pack at all. As they flew by us on the trail, waving in a particularly carefree way, I thought, *I wonder what it would be like to do this hike without forty-four pounds on my back...*

That is the essential question of Step #1. Selling is much easier, and you can be much more productive, if you handle negative thoughts and fears about sales *before* you hit the streets, or the phones.

WHY BOTHER? TALES FROM THE BAGGAGE CLAIM

What's the big deal about clearing up negative attitudes and fears? Why bother with the baggage? Isn't it best just to let sleeping dogs lie? Maybe, but the problem is that sooner or later, the dogs wake up.

Bob sells homes for a developer and got to be friends with some of the builders at the company. Over lunch, he listened to them grouse about how the developer made them cut corners on construction, use cheap materials, and build homes that were going to be in trouble five years down the road. Bob began to believe what they said and, over the next two quarters, his results went down 13%. Not only that, but his normally sunny approach to selling began to sour.

He told me his concerns about the construction and the developer's "unethical" approach. I asked him if he'd checked out what the builders were saying, and he had not. That was his first assignment. When people aren't happy in their work—and this particular group of builders definitely was not happy—they can start seeing everything through that filter. Bob had bought their opinions and interpretations hook, line and sinker, without ever finding out if they were actually true.

To make a very long story short, it turned out that the construction and developer's ethics were both up to Bob's standards. The builders had some serious issues about their salaries and contracts, and they had let those valid, but unrelated, issues spill over into their talk about boards and nails.

"That was a hard lesson," Bob said. "I thought I could just sell, no matter what I felt or thought about the product. I had no idea something like that would eat into my numbers so badly. The month after I found out the truth, my numbers went up 15%."

Most of us are carrying around much more psychological baggage than we realize. It's like trying to run a marathon with an extra thirty pounds around the waist. Having the courage to deal with our baggage gives us as much of a boost as losing that thirty pounds would give a marathoner. But without a system, it can be as difficult to keep current with our baggage as it can be to lose that thirty pounds. We know we should do it, but it's so easy to let it slip if we don't have a reminder in place. Step #1 is that reminder. It keeps us current with our own internal cleanup, so that we can sell with ease and aplomb.

YOUR SALES "OIL CHANGE"

Yeah, yeah, I know I should change my oil every 3,000 miles or three months. But it costs time and money, to say nothing of trying to *remember* when it's been 3,000 or three months! Plus, it's not fair that oil has to be changed, and I have more important things to do.

My brother does Customer Service at a large automobile dealership, and takes a dim view of my complaints. He once gave me a blow-by-blow description of what happens to the engines of cars owned by "oil arrogant" people like me. It was hair-raising—so now I change my oil on time, whether or not I want to, or think I should have to do so.

I make the same argument with people who don't want to look at their psychological baggage about selling. Some people figure they are "beyond all that." They say they've been selling a long time, are doing well, and can't be bothered with all that "woo woo" stuff.

Have you ever caught yourself thinking, *But I did the dishes yesterday! This is so unfair!* Or, *I shaved yesterday!* But like shaving and doing the dishes, keeping your poor brain free from negative thoughts and feelings about selling is an ongoing process.

I am astounded at the squirrelly little thoughts I catch darting across my mind from time to time. If I'm not vigilant about them, I pay a price. That price might be that I don't enjoy selling as much, that my self-esteem takes a beating, or that I don't get the results I want. But one way or another, I'll pay. It's a lot easier to clean up my attitudes *before* I start talking to people. It can even be interesting.

A year ago, I started talking to a woman about my seminar, and caught myself thinking, *She's too young. She won't want it and wouldn't get it anyway. When you're that age, you can sell running on raw energy.* Then I caught myself and thought, *That's ridiculous! Where did that thought come from?* (Hel-*lo*! When *I* was that young, *I* sold running on raw energy.)

If I hadn't caught that thought running wild in my brain, it could have affected how I talked to the woman. The baggage that I brought to the conversation might well have impacted her decision. As it turns out, I was dead wrong about her. That bright, ambitious young woman came to the seminar with almost no hesitation, had a great time, got value, and even wrote me a thank-you note. If I hadn't been alert to the baggage I was carrying and put it down, there might have been an entirely different outcome.

Where does this chatter come from? How can we unearth it, and what can we do about it?

WHERE DOES THE BAGGAGE COME FROM?

Our negative baggage comes from everywhere. It's a 360-degree bombardment. The good news is that it doesn't have to affect us if we *know it's there*, and *understand how to handle it*. By the end of this chapter, you'll have the skills to do both those things.

Some sources of negative baggage about selling are:

Ghosts from the past

A huge chunk of baggage comes from any bad, embarrassing, or limiting experiences you've had in the past, either as a *seller* or as a *buyer*. How was your experience of selling Girl Scout cookies? Or tickets to the school play? Or newspaper or magazine subscriptions? Did you ever find yourself the day before the raffle with a fistful of tickets you'd promised to sell? Did you ever pressure anyone to buy anything? How did it feel?

My friend Mary sold ad space in her nonprofit's magazine, and was not doing very well. Worse, she was having a terrible time. When she began examining her baggage, she recalled a series of chilling incidents from parochial grammar school. Every year, the school conducted a fundraising drive for overseas missions. Most kids hit up their parents. Mary's mother was very critical of this practice, and each year the fundraising drive became a catalyst that kicked up all sorts of family problems. Her mother would scream and criticize the school mercilessly for a week. It was nightmarish and humiliating for Mary, and that shame carried over into selling ad space for the nonprofit.

Each time she set out to sell, her normally sunny and warm presence turned a little brittle, and she didn't seem entirely genuine. People responded accordingly, and she only got minimal results. Mary used the tools in this chapter to turn her situation around. It took courage and perseverance, but she thought it was well worth the effort because, "I can be myself now. I'm getting much better results, and I'm having fun."

Baggage can also come from negative experiences as buyers. Have you ever been bothered by telemarketers? What did you think of them? What kind of people did you imagine them to be? Were you ever pressured to buy something? How did you feel? One woman said, "I have such contempt for those people on the phone. The thought of people thinking about *me* the way I think about *them* is agonizing! I'd rather not even have my own business than face that."

Where in your past did you pick up baggage? What beliefs did you form about selling?

Society's attitudes: What people hand us

Another chunk of baggage comes from family, friends and society at large. What did your parents say about salespeople? What did you think of people who sold for a living? When and where did you first hear about "used car salesmen"? How did you picture them? Did you ever encounter pushy ladies at the cosmetics counter, or Type A real estate agents? What jokes or slams have you heard about people who sell? Do you think people believe that selling is an honorable profession? Do you believe that it is?

The conventional wisdom is that whenever someone is selling, they're out to take you for a ride. Many of us approach buying with skepticism, and sometimes even with animosity. It's no wonder that when we go out to sell, we're afraid other people will approach *us* with skepticism or animosity. When we are concerned that people are going to see us that way, we often show up as defensive or apologetic. Even if we manage to hide the defensiveness fairly well, people usually sense "a tremor in the force." When they sense that something is wrong, or that we are not 100% behind ourselves, they are less likely to buy—and that confirms our worst fears.

Our own projections

Projections occur when we have an attitude, feeling, or thought—but we don't really want to have it, or don't want to admit we have it, and so we decide (consciously or unconsciously) that it's actually going on with someone else. It's not us! It's *them*! If I'm angry, for instance, I might look at the woman in the next lane of traffic while we're stopped at the light, and think, *That woman looks angry!* That's projection. Based on little or no information, we decide that what is going on with us is really going on with someone else.

We might think, for instance, *That person is depressed. He won't buy today.* In fact, we may be depressed. Or we might say, "She's having a bad day," when actually we're the one having a bad day. This is what I did with that young woman I decided wasn't going to take my seminar. I projected on to her my own feelings when I was her age, and made that my reality—even though it was completely untrue.

When we don't catch ourselves making projections, we just sail forth, convinced that we know what other people are thinking and feeling. We behave as if our projections were actually true, and often launch into interactions that are doomed to confusion and disappointment. And people decide whether or not to buy based on those interactions.

For instance, Ralph had a thin streak of stinginess. One day when he was in a foul mood anyway, a woman strolled into the computer store with a pinched frown on her face. Ralph decided she was stingy, and turned her over to the new guy. The woman bought a computer for herself, and another to surprise her son when he came home from college. She had simply had a headache that day, which accounted for her "pinched frown." Who knew? Not Ralph, who was out two commissions.

When we project our thoughts and feelings on to other people, we do both them and ourselves a disservice. We don't stay open to new interpretations, or to objective observations of what is truly going on.

Stuff we make up

Sometimes the baggage is just stuff we make up. It comes from nowhere except our own creative minds, perhaps seasoned with a pinch of projection and a whisper of fear about selling. It sounds crazy, but we simply make things up in our heads, based on nothing, then go out into the world and act as if they were absolutely true.

There was a time when I sold seminars on the phone for six to eight hours each day. From time to time, I went a little stir crazy. Sometimes I would just decide, based on nothing other than the sound of someone's voice, that he didn't want what I was selling. I'd rattle through my pitch, knowing I was doing a bad job but just wanting to get it over as quickly as possible so I could get on to the next person.

I'll never forget the first time one of these people interrupted me. "You don't really have to do this," he said. I froze, embarrassed to be caught in such bad behavior. "I've already decided I want it. What do I have to give you?" He was so intent on buying that he had been oblivious to my bad presentation. That was a good thing for me, but I was mortified.

Dodging that bullet was a good lesson. My negative thinking had resulted in an interaction that was less than honoring. It was just dumb luck that I got a good result. It was like watching a tennis ball slap into the top of the net on my side, then dribble over into my opponent's court. All I could do was promise myself to behave better in the future, and be particularly good to that poor guy.

Plain old fear

Baggage originates in fear, and generates fear. Fear that we'll be too pushy, or too docile, or that we're just not powerful enough to get results. Or that we *are* powerful, but can't be trusted to treat people well. We're afraid of our own inadequacies, or our own brilliance, or of what people will think of us. We're afraid we'll be rejected. Or do better than somebody we love. Or that we won't speak in an articulate or persuasive way about our product or service. Or that we're not prepared, or not eloquent speakers anyway. A surprising number of people are afraid that there is some huge, mysterious secret to selling that everybody else knows, but they don't.

Fear is normal, in selling and in life. But when we don't unearth and name those fears, they become congealed and solid. They start insisting that we carry them around all day. They demand attention and soothing—and they see that if they whine or yell at us, they get even more attention. Before long, we are focusing more on them than we are on our results, or the joy of offering people something that we value.

WHAT DOES IT DO?

What actually happens when we lug around all those negative decisions and opinions, past experiences and mental chatter? The problems arise in four phases:

1. We don't see people or situations clearly.

Our muscles ache from carrying that heavy baggage, so we tend to be a little cranky. Plus, we can get twisted into some strange positions when we're carrying all that weight. The result is that frequently we're seeing people and circumstances from odd angles. We see only what our position allows us to see—not what's actually there.

In sales, that spells disaster. Not only do we need to see what is really there, but we need to see it through the *buyer's* eyes, as well as our own. When we are carrying heavy baggage, we can't do that.

2. We speak with people based on these false perceptions.

When we see from a false angle, we act from a false angle. If we think people are going to look down on us, we act as if they are going to look down on us. That might mean we show up as shy, defensive, surly, or whatever our individual proclivities suggest. If we think people are jerks and not going to buy from us, then that's how we come into the situation.

Genuine, present-time appreciation of people goes out the window. Reality goes out the window. Respect for ourselves and our product goes out the window. All we have is what's in the suitcase.

Remember Ralph, who projected his own stingy streak onto the woman who walked into the computer store? Because he hadn't put down his baggage, he interacted with her by dismissing her, and turning her over to the new guy. *The cost*: Commissions on two computers. *The hidden cost*: While the new guy was taking his wife out for a steak dinner that night, Ralph was beating himself up and wondering whether he was going to make his quota.

3. People react to our baggage-based behavior.

We don't usually show up at our best when we relate to people based on nothing more than old ideas, fears and projections. And understandably, people react to us accordingly. They came to buy, or at least to find out about what we're selling. They expect and deserve our best. When they don't get it, sometimes they take it personally.

Angela was the golden girl at her insurance office. In her first two years, she had sold more than anyone—even the veterans. Some folks at the firm were happy for her, but others were resentful. The atmosphere at the office was sticky with tension. Rather than deal with it in a straightforward way, Angela began to "figure out" what was happening. (Translation: She began to make wholesale decisions about people and circumstances based on nothing more than surmise and projection.) Without talking to anybody except her friends, who were happy to collude with her, she decided that people at the firm had made a pact against her. She "realized" that they were out to get her, and were undercutting her in many devious ways. If she wasn't vigilant, she decided, they would cut her to ribbons within six months.

Angela developed not just a chip on her shoulder, but a redwood—and some of her attitude bled into her interactions with clients. Where she had once been assertive, she became aggressive. Where she had once been clear, she began to push ethical borders. She was short with clients because she thought she needed to sell more, more quickly, in order to counteract the coup. She no longer had the patience to fool around with people who needed some time to move through impediments to buying.

Clients started to back off. They didn't like dealing with Angela. They didn't like being "shoved around" by someone who was supposed to be working for *them*, for God's sake. Who did she think she was? They got defensive with her. Some even met her baggage-based behavior with their own aggression and got rid of her. Word got around, and Angela didn't get as many referrals as she had been getting.

When Angela did Step #1, it took a while to clean up the mess this baggage had caused. But she got the lesson. When you bring your own baggage to a situation, you almost always set off someone else's baggage. And often, that person is your potential customer.

4. Our baggage is validated when they don't buy.

We stagger into the sales arena under the weight and torque of all our baggage. We make decisions about people based on nothing more than what's in the suitcase, and then speak to them as if it were true. They react to us based on that. Frequently, the result is not good. The fact that they don't buy reinforces our baggage—and we're off into the next sale, lugging around the same old suitcases.

People usually don't make their decision to buy, or not to buy, solely on the basis of their relationship with us. But it has an impact, and there is no point in allowing that impact to be negative. The bottom line is this: If we show up squirrelly, they are less likely to buy. There is just no point in setting ourselves up that way.

WHAT CAN YOU DO? THE FOUR CHECKPOINTS

Don't be discouraged! As uncomfortable as it is to look at all this baggage, putting it down is actually quite easy.

Step #1 has four checkpoints. They are simple, powerful ways to keep baggage from getting in your way. Sometimes you need to step systematically through each checkpoint. Other times, they all happen in the twinkling of an eye. Even if your baggage seems to disappear the minute you identify what it is in Checkpoint 1, go through the other checkpoints to be sure you've gotten it all.

CHECKPOINT 1: IDENTIFY THE MENTAL CHATTER.

When you allow mental chatter to natter on and on, you often start to believe what it says. You see it not as mental chatter running on at the mouth, but as reality. You start to think that people and situations really are the way mental chatter says they are. That's not a good place from which to sell.

The minute you write down what mental chatter is saying, you see it for what it is—mental chatter, and not reality. You've put it outside yourself. It may still be there, but it can't cause as much trouble. You can still buy into it if you choose to do so, but now you have a choice. Just be a scribe. As mental chatter rattles on, simply write down what it says. After a few minutes, you may even find yourself amused.

One morning I had a phone appointment about a large contract, and I got this idea that the woman I was to call simply didn't like me. I have no idea where it came from, but there it was. My mental chatter rambled on matter-of-factly that she didn't have anything against the seminar; she simply didn't like me as a person. The result was, of course, that I didn't want to make the call. So I proceeded to Checkpoint 1. I wrote down all the snaky little thoughts that were running around in my mind: *She doesn't like people who are successful sellers—or tall people, because she's so short. She hates me because I dress differently from how she does, and she wants to stick it to me.*

After about five minutes of this, I had to laugh. I had absolutely no basis in fact for any of it. I was making it all up in my head—possibly because I really wanted that contract, and was unconsciously constructing an excuse in case I didn't get it. I wanted to be able to say the deal fell though because she just didn't like me. In fact, I was completely wrong about everything. She could not have been more gracious or generous, and it was an uplifting conversation as well as a successful deal.

Often, writing down the mental chatter is all you need to do. When you define it, put it outside yourself, and take a good look at it, you take dominion over it.

CHECKPOINT 2: CHECK TO SEE IF IT'S TRUE.

For each piece of mental chatter you identify in Checkpoint 1, ask yourself if it's true. You may have to do some research, as Bob did with the home developer whose builders were upset with him. Most of the mental chatter that rattles around in our heads isn't true. But as Bob discovered, you need to check it out if you have any doubts.

When Anne did Checkpoint 1, she wrote down this piece of mental chatter about herself: *When push comes to shove and I'm up against a quota or promise, I'll slime out on people and do anything to get the sale.* When that thought was rolling around in her brain, it felt very real. But the minute she wrote it down, she told me, "I felt silly. Yes, the fear was real. But then I asked myself, *C'mon, is this really true?* I saw that of course it wasn't. It was just a fear. Mental chatter wanted me to stay where I was, and that particular thought did the trick! Until I got it up into the light and took a good look at it, it had me paralyzed."

Most of the time, you'll see right away that the chatter is not true. But what if it *is* true?! Simple. Fix it, if you can.

CHECKPOINT 3: FIX WHAT YOU CAN.

Is there anything in the chatter that really does need your attention? Is there something about your product that needs fixing? To whom should you speak about it? Do you resent someone at work for an old offense that is still bothering you and getting in your way of doing a good job? Is there something about your own business—accounting practices, quality control, customer service—that needs fine-tuning in order for you to feel good about getting out there and selling it?

If you see something that needs to be fixed or cleaned up, do so.

▶ Terry's financial records were a mess. She realized that, on some level, she didn't want any more clients in her therapy practice because that would just compound the mess. She fixed the situation by hiring someone to help her get her finances and records in order. That opened the door, psychologically, and clients began flooding in.

▶ Chuck sold magnet jewelry as a multi-level marketer. He realized that his mental chatter centered on a fear that he was too far down the line ever to make a good living. He put aside a whole weekend to crunch numbers. His goal was to answer these questions:

✓ Exactly how much do I need to make each month in order to "make a good living"?

✓ How much product do I need to sell, and how much down-line do I need to put in place, in order to make that amount?

✓ What do I need to do to sell that amount of product and get that much down-line?

✓ Am I willing to do that?

They were brilliant questions. (In fact, I have recommended Chuck's questions to many people who are making the choice to stay in a selling situation or to cut their losses and leave it.) Chuck even invited an accountant friend over for dinner Saturday night to go over the figures with him—another brilliant idea. He saw that he could make it work, and that he wanted to do so.

Prior to that weekend, Chuck had not been playing full out with his business. He made a stab at selling each day, but he felt uncertain, resentful and uncommitted. When he decided to fix his condition by digging in and getting the facts, everything cleared up. He knew where he was going and how to get there.

What needs fixing?

Things that need fixing usually involve ethical issues, logistical problems, or just getting accurate facts. The logistical problems, like Terry's financial records, are often the easiest to fix. Getting accurate facts just means digging in, as Chuck did. It can be uncomfortable to start that process, but everything becomes clear once the information emerges.

The stickiest wicket involves ethical issues. If your own ethics are in question, you're lucky. You are in control, and can simply set things right. If you are fudging on your consulting time or on your statistics, for instance, you can simply stop doing it. If your company's ethics are in question, you may or may not be able to rectify the situation. First, check to see if your suspicions are actually true, as Bob did with the home developer. If there really is a problem, see if you are in a position to fix it. If you can't change how things are done, you have a choice. You can get out, or let it go and live with it. Neither is comfortable, but at least you know where you stand.

CHECKPOINT 4: SWITCH CHANNELS.

If mental chatter still seems to be running your show even after you've identified it, checked out its truth level, and fixed it, then move on to Checkpoint 4: Switch channels. Switching channels is actually very easy; the trick is *remembering to do it*.

Why switch? You get what you focus on.

If you focus on the negative chatter, that's where your energy goes. That is what has the power. If you focus on something else, you change the flow of energy and power to that thing—whether it's your daughter's wedding, world events, tuna fish, or the fabulous sales results you want. When you give energy to mental chatter, you are inviting it to take over.

If you've decided you want to switch channels, here is how to do it:

How to switch channels

Mental chatter is just one frequency, or channel, on the radio in our minds. You switch channels simply by focusing your attention elsewhere on the dial. Here's how it works. Right now, you are looking at a book. Now look up at the wall. You just switched channels. You can choose the thoughts on which you focus, just as you can choose whether to look at the book or at the wall. Switching your attention away from negative mind chatter is just that simple. And it can become just that easy, with practice.

Almost any other channel will do—friends or family, a book you're reading, a pleasant memory, baseball scores, or the delightful frequencies you'll discover in Step #2. You simply nod politely to mental chatter, recognizing its existence but not giving it much attention, and then look elsewhere.

As you become adept at switching channels, mental chatter is less likely to snag you. As you listen more to other channels—ones that might be playing self-esteem, positive anticipation, or enjoyment—you notice mental chatter less. Trying to fight mental chatter, and make it go away, is about as effective as trying to make a radio channel go away. It is a waste of energy. Just accept it in the same way that you accept having blue, green, brown, or hazel eyes—and focus elsewhere.

Here are some tools to help:

TOOLS FOR SWITCHING CHANNELS

When you have decided to switch channels, choose one or all of these tools:

1. *Create a Choice.* Get out the list you made in Checkpoint 1 of everything mental chatter is saying. Next to each piece of chatter, in a column just to the right of it, write down an alternative positive thought, feeling, belief, or opinion. In column #1, you might find: "I'm afraid of selling." The alternative positive feeling might be: "I'm going to have fun with this today, and put myself in charge." It doesn't matter what you write down as an alternative statement, and it doesn't matter which statement you believe more strongly. Just putting them down, as two sides of the same coin, will take some of the charge off the chatter. You see that the mental chatter was just one of several points of view you could adopt.

2. *Your best vision.* When you hear mental chatter's footsteps in the back of your mind, or find yourself caught up in the quagmire of negativity, write a paragraph describing what you want selling to be like for you that day. You might write: "Today I'm going to have selling be about serving the people I contact. I'm going to appreciate them, talk to as many as needed to keep my promise, and have

fun. I'll take a break about eleven o'clock, but otherwise I'm going to stick with it and give it my all." Again, it doesn't matter whether or not you believe what you write. You're just snapping yourself out of the trance in which mental chatter has caught you.

3. *Physical prompts.* People have told me they put "Switch channels" on their screen savers, or stickers on their computers or phones that remind them to refocus toward results and having fun. One woman got shiny red apple stickers and put them around the edges of her computer monitor to remind her that, "An apple a day keeps the chatter away." Okay, okay. It may sound corny, but believe me, we would all be very happy with her numbers! What works for you? People have put on their desks as reminders: stones they've gathered on vacations, purple feathers from cat toys, pyramids, candles and a variety of objects that might seem strange to the rest of us. The point is that when you look at your physical prompt, you can do a quick scan to make sure your thoughts haven't taken you down a road you don't want to travel.

4. *Sit in another chair.* Sometimes changing your perspective physically helps change your perspective psychologically or emotionally. I learned this tool from John, who said, "I don't care how it looks. Guys in my office looked at me funny when I started, but then they saw it worked for me. Now, when they see me doing it, their eyes get wide because they know I'm coming back *ready*." Give this tool permission to work for you, and it will.

5. *Walk around the block.* When the chatter gets loud and nothing else seems to work, take a walk around the block. It's a stronger version of changing your chair.

6. *Call a friend*—someone with whom you've discussed the Soul of Selling and who supports you in sticking with it. When you get your friend on the phone, *do not* ask that person to collude with you. Then mental chatter has you both in its clutches! Begin the conversation with, "I'm calling you because mental chatter's got me and I want to break its hold. Let me tell you what it's saying, and I don't want you to agree with it…"

7. *Inspiration.* Keep something inspirational on your desk—a book, a symbol, a saying, a few paragraphs of writing by someone you admire. Let its energy fill you if you begin to lose steam.

8. *Project yourself into the future.* Imagine what it will be like after you've produced the results, and enjoy how great it feels. Create a visual image, and then let it fill with emotion.

"I'd rather fight than switch."

Benson & Hedges cigarettes used to advertise with pictures of men, women, even dogs sporting black eyes. Beneath the photos was the phrase: "I'd rather fight than switch."

It worked because the photo was unexpected, but also because people recognized a part of themselves in the ad. We all have times when we know we aren't on track, but we'd rather fight than switch. We'd rather be right about where we are than be happy, or productive, or rich, or relaxed. We don't want to switch—or even examine—the points of view, attitudes, beliefs and mental chatter that are holding us back, but that are part of how we define ourselves. At least, we don't want to do it *now*.

Momma said there'd be days like this, and there are. Sometimes we just throw ourselves into the well, and give ourselves over to mental chatter. We feel sorry for ourselves, get angry with the people around us, and sink into depression about our agonizing situation. We've all done it, and we'll do it again. It's just good to know that when we're tired of doing that, we have an alternative.

You can't switch channels if your feet are dug in, any more than you can make another person switch channels if they don't want to do so. If nothing seems to be working when you are in the grasp of mental chatter, ask yourself whether you're a candidate for the Benson & Hedges ad.

CHECKING YOUR BAGGAGE

Enough theory! Let's get down to business and see what your baggage looks like, so you can let it go and reclaim your power from it. As we've seen, negative mental chatter usually gravitates toward four areas:

- ▶ Selling in general
- ▶ You as a seller
- ▶ Your product or service
- ▶ Your contacts

It's easiest to tackle these areas one at a time.

Selling in General

Begin by making a list titled "My ideas about selling in general." Then write down all the dark, squirrelly things you think, or have ever thought, about selling. Search out all the imagined reasons not to do it, the reasons you don't or can't succeed, all your worries and fears, and all the proof mental chatter offers that what you have just written is true.

Be thorough, and don't edit your answers. If something flickers across your mind, write it down—whether or not you really believe it, and whether or not you think it has any impact on you.

Here are some questions to get you going:

▶ What are the most uncomfortable things about selling?
▶ What do you hate the most?
▶ When do you feel the worst?
▶ Why is selling so hard?
▶ What are the worst things about selling?

Some answers people have given are:

▶ It's sleazy. My mother would turn over in her grave if she knew I was doing this.
▶ You're always lying, one way or another. Nothing's as good as you have to tell people it is to get them to buy.
▶ It's difficult, and if there were anything else on earth to do I'd be running for it.
▶ Only people without a conscience can sell.

We all have our own variations on these themes. What are yours?

▶ _____
▶ _____

Good for you! Now let's look at the next category of baggage.

You as a Seller

Make another list titled "My ideas about myself as a seller." Now write down all your negative thoughts, feelings and fears about yourself as a seller. Be sure to include all your "wounds." Remember, the purpose of these exercises is to bring to the surface any thoughts or fears that are skulking around in your unconscious. This is no time to be nice. Unearthing this baggage takes courage, but it's well worth it.

Here are some questions to get you started:

▶ Why are you not a good seller?
▶ What gets in the way for you?
▶ Why are you unsuited to selling?

Some answers people have given are:

▶ I'm too scared. The thought of setting a goal and having to make it just makes me crazy.
▶ I don't talk well when I'm pressured, and I don't know what to say.
▶ I don't want to be rejected or humiliated. I get angry when these things happen.

What are your thoughts about yourself as a seller?

▶ _____
▶ _____

It's not easy to look directly at these fears and suspicions, untrue as they may be. You're doing a great job. The next category, please!

Your Product or Service

Next, consider any baggage you may have lurking around in your mind about the product or service you offer. Title this third list "My ideas about my product or service." Then write down any doubts, concerns, criticisms, or niggling fears you have about your product or service. These don't need to be big concerns. In fact, it's often little concerns, the kind you don't think you need to do anything about, that get in the way.

Use these questions to keep on track:

▶ What bothers you about the product?
▶ What inadequacies do you see in it?
▶ Is there anything that you think might disappoint people, or that you don't think is ethical?
▶ Anything you don't understand?
▶ Anything you don't like?

These are some frequent answers to these questions:

▶ I know that people can get a better loan rate elsewhere.
▶ I know people bring back this phone over and over.
▶ There's something I don't understand about the contract.
▶ I don't know that much about financing the cars, so I check out when it comes to that—making it, like, you know, hard to close.

What are your thoughts about your product or service?

▶ _____

▶ _____

When you are finished, ask yourself if there is anything else about your product or service that gives you pause. Be 100% whistle clean with what you are offering people, or it will come back to bite you. Onward to your contacts!

Your Buyers or Contacts

This is the most important area, and it's a tricky one. The Soul of Selling is about respecting, honoring and appreciating these people—but you are in a vulnerable position with them. In the end, they hold all the cards. They can say "No." Their capacity to influence your outcomes makes mental chatter crazy. You want to reach out to them, but mental chatter usually kicks up some fear about what they will do "to" you. Mental chatter wants to convince you that this is an adversarial relationship in which somebody wins and somebody loses, and you had better win!

The Soul of Selling is not about winning or losing. It is about you coming to selling with a clean slate, inspired by your personal values, clear about what you're going to say, committed to serving people and giving them everything they need to buy—but promising that you will respect, honor and appreciate them regardless of what they choose. You are in a better position to serve and honor people when you have anticipated what mental chatter might say about them.

At the top of your fourth list, write: "My ideas about my contacts." Ask yourself these questions to get the juices flowing:

▶ What are your worst fears about these people?
▶ Do you have any fears or concerns about them?
▶ What would you hate most?
▶ What bad behavior have you encountered in the past?
▶ What bad behavior do you imagine that you'll encounter in the future?
▶ What else might be negative about them?

Here are some answers people have given:

▶ They don't want to buy, but will pity me and then will patronize me.
▶ They'll return it and then make me wrong for having forced them to buy it.

▶ I'll never be able to face them again, because they'll know I've used them.

▶ They won't like me, even if they like the product.

▶ They just want to watch me dance for them. Then they'll walk away.

What are your worst thoughts and fears about the people you will contact?

▶ _____

▶ _____

Congratulations! You've just done yourself, your product or service, your contacts, and the entire world of selling a favor. Everything is going to be easier because you've taken the time to identify these thoughts, fears and opinions. Just saying what they are takes away at least half their power over you—and over your results.

WHAT NOW?

What do you do once you've written all this down? First, give yourself a pat on the back for completing Checkpoint 1 of Step #1. You've dissolved a huge chunk of baggage, just by bringing it up into the light.

Next, you just march through Checkpoints 2, 3 and 4. Start with Checkpoint 2 and ask yourself if any of this mental chatter is true. If any of it is, go to Checkpoint 3 and fix what you can. Then activate Checkpoint 4 and switch channels. Refocus your attention away from the baggage, and toward your promises.

In the next chapter, we'll look at how to find the most productive channels on the dial.

EXERCISES

EXERCISE #1: Complete the exercises in this chapter to identify your baggage in the four areas: selling in general, yourself as a seller, your product or service, and your contacts.

EXERCISE #2: For each item you discover, ask yourself whether or not there is any truth to what mental chatter is saying.

EXERCISE #3: If there is something you can do to correct a situation that is bothering you, make a list of everything you need to do. Then do it.

CHAPTER 6

Step #2:
Pinpoint Your Passions

When I was a young woman in Chicago, most people I knew lived in walkup apartments with hardwood floors. Every so often, you had to strip these floors. It was a drag, but if you didn't do it the wax would build up and the new coat wouldn't go on properly. So on Saturday mornings all over the city, my friends and I would apply ourselves to this chore. When the stripping was over, you looked out on a clean, beautiful floor spread out before you, ready for a new coat of wax. That was the fun part. I used to love laying down that fresh, brilliant, shiny coat of wax. It was delicious and satisfying.

Step #1 is like stripping hardwood floors, and Step #2 is like laying down the gleaming new layer of wax. You clear away what you don't want, and put in place something that brings joy to you and to others. These two steps give you a rich, fertile foundation for all the rest of the Soul of Selling.

BRINGING THE SPARKLE

Step #2 is about bringing the sparkle to selling—for you and for your buyers. It's about taking the time and energy to discover what you find personally valuable and genuinely exciting about your product or service, your contacts, selling in general, and yourself as a seller. These are the same four areas you cleaned up in Step #1. You put down your baggage and swept out all the negativity. That was an enormous step, but you can't just leave a void. If you don't replace those old fears and mental chatter with something positive, the negativity will start creeping back in.

In Step #2, you fill each of those four areas with treasure. I'm not talking about just ticking down an old dog-eared list of benefits; I'm talking about being inspired in a way that gets you out of bed in the morning. This step is about bringing life, passion and sparkle to everyone and everything involved in your selling process.

Helen Keller said, "Life is either a daring adventure, or nothing." The same is true of selling. When you know what genuinely excites you, you can sell from a place of authentic passion.

THE REFRIGERATOR: BEFORE PICTURE

Say that you're buying your first new refrigerator. You have a general idea of what you want, but the fridge that you're replacing was fifteen years old. You don't know what's new, or exactly where you fit into today's world of refrigerators. You wander into the appliance department slowly, maybe even sideways, and start checking things out. From somewhere behind the washer/dryers, the salesperson appears before you.

"What can I help you with today?" he booms.

You give him a general idea of your needs, and the size you want. You ask about the extra cost of getting ivory instead of white.

"I've got just the fridge for you," he says, and pulls you over to a model that seems to fill your needs. He runs down a list of features and benefits. You can almost see him reading it in his mind. "Yeah, it's a great model. This is the one you want," he finishes, and glances over to the vacuum cleaners.

The refrigerator does seem to fill your needs. It has the features you want, and the cost of ivory isn't astronomical. Yet you don't feel like buying. You still have a sense there may be things you don't know about buying refrigerators, things you *should* know. And if that's the case, you're pretty sure this guy isn't going to tell you what those things are. You thank him for his time, and leave to shop elsewhere. After making the rounds, you discover that the model he showed you really is the one you want. You buy it from someone else.

Many things went wrong in this sale, but in this chapter we will focus on how the salesperson told you about the benefits.

THE REFRIGERATOR: AFTER PICTURE

I actually did buy a refrigerator last year. The man who helped me was a living, breathing paragon of Step #2: Pinpoint your passions.

As I inched down the long row of refrigerators, trying to look as if I were pondering the deeper aspects of refrigerator selection, I'm sure a sign appeared over my head with an arrow pointing down at me and the words: "This woman is looking for something 'cute,' and has *no clue* what she's doing."

I found a refrigerator I liked just as the salesman appeared and introduced himself. (Okay, it was cute.) I told him what I wanted, summarized my short, unhappy history with refrigerators, and gestured vaguely toward the model in question, saying, "This is nice."

Small lines appeared between his eyes. He pursed his lips, nodded noncommittally, and said nothing. I leaned in and asked, "What's wrong with it?"

I'd explained about the questionable wiring in my building, and some unpleasant encounters I'd had with other electronic devices. It must have been clear to him that I was not someone with whom anything should be left to chance or skill. He was mentally putting all this together with the model I showed him, and not liking what he saw.

"Come here," he said conspiratorially, leading me over to another model. He opened the freezer and looked at me significantly, as if I'd better listen up. He very slowly and deliberately explained how, in this new model, the freezer design ensured that if the electricity went off, melting water wouldn't leak down into the motor. He explained what *that* meant, and then took me back to "my" model. He showed me how it didn't have this freezer feature, and indicated with his finger the path that the water would take into the motor.

Our eyes met in horror. We were both picturing the refrigerator blowing up, and we both knew I was just the gal who could do it.

"Thank you so much," I said, touching his arm. The "safe" model was slightly less than the other, and I could not wait to give him my credit card.

He didn't have to give me that electronics lesson, but it was clear that he wanted me to have the real skinny on both models. And it wasn't just that one was safer than the other, although that would have been enough for me. As he was showing me the safer model, he spoke of it almost lovingly and ran his hand over the curved piece of plastic in the freezer that staved off disaster. He admired that. It meant something to him personally. He was also willing to go the extra mile for someone who was electronically impaired. He must have known he had an easy sale in the first model I showed him, and he risked losing that sale to show me the second model. He honored the profession of selling enough to help me above and beyond the call of duty, and he honored himself enough to be authentic and tell the truth.

I knew I was dealing with an honest person who knew what he was doing, genuinely admired his product, was giving me his very best and wanted me to be happy with my decision. He had a personal investment in the product, in how he interacted with me and handled the sale, and in himself as a man of honor. I was instinctively comfortable with buying from him—and I bought. I walked away happy with him, with myself, and with my purchase. I would seek out that guy, and his store, again.

This is the power of presenting your product or service with authentic, personal passion.

PASSION IS *INTENTIONAL*

We've all had moments when passion just appeared, without our having to create it. The enthusiasm was just there, inspired by a person, event, situation, or sunset. Spontaneous passion happens, but you can't count on it. Spontaneous passion is great for romance, spirituality, the arts and many other aspects of life. It's not so great for selling, though, because you can't count on it to show up at the same time that your customers do.

The good news is that passion doesn't have to be spontaneous. It can also be *intentional*. You can call it forth at will, at the exact times you want it. You don't need luck, karma, or lightning striking in just the right place. You don't have to sit around waiting for it. You can bring it to any situation, whenever you want to do so.

New sellers often say, "I just don't have the enthusiasm today. I'm not inspired." You never again have to use those words. In fact, it's part of the Soul of Selling *not* to say those words—but rather, to reach down and *find* the sparkle. *Find* the inspiration and passion.

This chapter will give you everything you need to create passion at will, and to make selling fun and exciting whenever you choose.

EAT THE FROSTING!

I used to eat the cake first. Then, with all the "hard work" done, I luxuriated in the frosting and spun myself into a sugar coma. There is another school of thought that suggests you eat the frosting first. It's what you wanted anyway. Once you satiate yourself with the frosting, you may not even be interested in eating the cake. Therefore, the whole experience becomes a slimming exercise.

There's some flaw in that logic, but I am not inclined to pursue it. The point is: Step #2 is the frosting. Go for it!

Cheryl left her office manager job and began selling commercial real estate in Honolulu. She blamed her slow start on the fact that it was a very competitive market. It was, but she agreed to use the Soul of Selling. She was diligent about Step #1, identifying her baggage and fixing what she could. She told me, "I've got it knocked now. That's all I have to do. Really. The good stuff you talk about in Step #2 is already there. This is Honolulu! All I have to do is look out the window!"

She went back out selling, but called me in a month. "I cleared out the old stuff, but it keeps coming back," she said. I suggested she do Step #2 and fill that void with positive material.

Cheryl's list of what she genuinely valued about selling started with "Make a lot of money." She followed with, "I get to drive all around this beautiful city" and "I love Hawaiian décor." The last item on her list was "I get to help people find great places of business that they love." When it came to herself as a seller, she began with, "I can make things happen when I have to" and worked up to "I'm good with people, I love this area, and I'm terrific with putting people together with places that will work for them."

She called me and said sheepishly, "Alright. I'm jazzed. I had a big smile on my face when I finished those lists. And yes, I can go 100% now!" Over the next six months, she increased her sales by 23%. It was enough to make her do Steps #3 through #6!

Allen, who took the seminar with his sales staff, had been selling insurance for twenty years. He knew he had to be creative in order to keep engaged in selling over the long haul, and saw the value of Step #2 immediately. He jumped into it and kept going, even during the breaks. He didn't stop until he had squeezed out every drop of value he could identify in all four areas. He even told me, "For people who've been doing this a long time, you should make them come up with at least four things in each area they've never thought of before." I pass this on to you.

Allen called me a month after the seminar and said, "You know, my results have gotten better, but the main thing is I'm having a lot more fun. I feel like I'm doing something exciting again. I look forward to going to work in the morning."

Step #2 carries a double value: You improve how you talk about your product or service, and you enjoy talking about it more. It's double passion, on demand!

WHAT STEP #2 GIVES YOU

What is the magic of Step #2? Why does it make such a difference to identify the specific personal values you see in each of the four categories? There are many reasons. Here are some, and you will probably discover others that are unique to you:

1. *You get more real and authentic.* You may think your product is great, but the value lives in you more vividly and genuinely, and is easier to articulate to your customers, if you sit down and write out exactly what you think is great about it—without referring to the pat answers your manager gave you. You may value things about your product or service that aren't even on the benefits list. Those very things may be your strongest selling points. They may be exactly the things your contacts find valuable, when they are pointed out. Even if they aren't, your contacts can be inspired by your enthusiasm and how much *you* love those things.

    The same is true of the three other categories. People say, "Hey, selling is great. I wouldn't be doing it if I didn't think that." But what is so great about it? The more specific you can be, the more real it becomes for you. It means more if you can say something as personal and specific as, "I like selling because it puts me out on the edge, and every day I become a bigger person because of that." Don't be shy about naming the specific strengths you bring to selling: "I want to give people what they want, and that makes me good at selling."

2. *You get more naturally enthusiastic.* The more deeply and clearly you touch what excites you, the more inspiring you are when you talk about your product, service, project, or vision. Your natural enthusiasm pervades everything you say.

3. *You are more original.* Do you know when people are just rattling down a list of features and benefits? Can you tell the difference

between mouthing the party line on a product, and speaking from personal enthusiasm? Other people can, too. Steve sold a three-day personal growth seminar. He gave people all the information about it, but they always lit up when he launched into his own personal value—the fact that he had spent three days away from his normal world and created a "retreat" for himself. He told how he had used that time to think about what he really wanted from his life and how he could re-ignite his relationship. People responded to that very personal value.

4. *You own what you are saying.* You may own it now, but you will own it even more strongly when you are the original source of what you're telling people. After Wade did Step #2 about the tools he sells, he told me, "I say almost the same things, but I say them real differently. It's coming from deeper inside now, and folks sense that. They listen differently."

5. *You're in the driver's seat.* Nobody is telling you, "Go out and say this or that." You may be saying what they suggest you say, but you are also adding your own value. You're not just connecting the dots somebody else drew on the paper; you're creating your own picture.

6. *You have a crib sheet.* Writing down your answers gives you a permanent record. You can come back to these pages if negativity starts to overtake you, and even use them as crib sheets when you talk to people.

Seasoned professionals sometimes groan about doing Step #2. "Been there, done that, got the T-shirt" appears in the bubbles over their heads. At first, you may believe you already know everything of value about what you are offering. I invite you to make these lists anyway. I have seen people unearth values they didn't even know they had about selling, about themselves, about their product or service, and especially about their contacts.

WHERE DO THE ANSWERS COME FROM?

Most of the answers are right beneath the surface, just waiting for the question to be asked. They float up easily when you take on the assignment to discover them, sit quietly for a few moments, and are ready to write down the answers.

You may want to ask your friends or colleagues for help in identifying your own value as a seller, or even in pinpointing the value of your product or service. It's easier to toot your own horn when somebody else is already playing that tune. Make your own lists, but then ask your friends or colleagues to add their opinions. Compare your lists. If you agree with what they say, use it. Including other people in this process also gives you an extra dimension of support.

Because the passion comes from within you, it is always available. If you ever feel your inspiration flagging, you can just go inside and get some more. You will always find more appreciation and enthusiasm, if you ask. You have an endless source of renewal.

MAKING STEP #2 WORK

Step #2 brings your values to the surface—but then you have to make them work for you. Here are three checkpoints to help you make the best use of Step #2:

Checkpoint 1: Identify the value.

You will make four lists, just as you did in Step #1:

- ▶ What I value about selling in general
- ▶ What I value about myself as a seller
- ▶ What I value about my product or service
- ▶ What I value about the people I will contact

I suggest you start with one area—it doesn't matter which one—and start writing. As you begin, thoughts about what you value in other areas will probably occur to you as well. It's as if, once you open that door, a whole new part of your mind opens up and your values come flooding out. Have all four lists handy, so that you don't lose any of it.

Your finished product is a set of four lists that lay out very clearly the specific things that you, personally, value in each of the four areas.

Checkpoint 2: Showcase your values.

What do you do with this information? Before you even start talking to people about it, you showcase it. Keep it in your line of sight. Display it prominently, if only for yourself. You may not want to hang big poster boards around your office, but get those papers into a special file on your desk or computer. Keep them before you in some way, and make them easy to access so you can read them at least once a day.

This information is one of your most important sales tools. When you switch channels, *this is one channel to which you'll be switching.* You want this "value bank" at your fingertips.

Here are some ways people have showcased the values they discovered:

▶ Print hard copies, and keep them in a beautiful folder on your desk. One woman used a deep red folder and put a gold star on it.
▶ Choose one value each day and put it on your screen saver.
▶ Print up your values in a special font and put them on or above your desk.
▶ Print "mini-versions" of your values, laminate them, and put them in your wallet or purse.
▶ Keep a copy on your bathroom mirror to review each morning.

The best way to showcase your values is the one you discover on your own. Again, what works for *you*? The point is to keep these passions real and alive for yourself, and to make them your foundation for each day of selling.

Checkpoint 3: Review and revise your values regularly.

Keep your values alive and fresh. That means revisiting them, and re-creating them, on a regular basis. The values you define in Checkpoint 1 may last a lifetime, or they may be outmoded in five minutes. The important thing is to keep an eye on them, and monitor whether or not they still inspire you. If the passion isn't there, redo Step #2—even if you did it ten minutes ago.

Revisit Step #2 at least once a month, whether or not you feel the need to do so. Add some new values and get rid of those that are no longer particularly inspiring. Your passions are your powerhouse. Make sure all the machinery is well maintained, nicely oiled, and used frequently.

Ready to jump in? Let's go through each of the four areas and define your personal values.

WHAT DO YOU LOVE?

Defining your values is similar to defining your baggage, only easier and more fun. You don't need to eliminate anything; you just need to encourage and promote thoughts that you already find pleasant.

Start with Checkpoint 1, and make your four lists. As you write, keep your answers as personal as you can. The computers you sell may have a high rating in *Consumer Reports*, but try to focus on what you like about them personally as well. It might be something you know about tech support, or simply that you find them particularly stylish. There's nothing wrong with these "trivial" preferences. They generate enthusiasm in you, and that inspiration can be infectious. Make your answers specific. For instance, the fountain pen you sell isn't just "good." It is great because even looking at it on your desk makes you feel successful.

Selling in General

This list includes everything you have ever found valuable about selling, or have thought might be valuable, or that you have *wanted* to find valuable. If you are a full-time seller with a billion-dollar sales goal, you might find different values from someone who has a two-month project to raise funds for a community organization—or you may not. What do you find valuable, or what are you *willing* to find valuable, in the activity of selling?

Here are some questions to get you started:

▶ What do you want the process of selling to do for you?
▶ What value have you gotten from selling in the past?
▶ What value have you seen other people get?
▶ What can you learn from selling?
▶ Of what value is that to you?

People have discovered these kinds of answers:

▶ Selling is a great way to become a more effective and compassionate person.
▶ Selling makes you powerful.
▶ Selling really asks you to get out there, and at the same time be good to people.
▶ Selling is a great way to make money because you can make more, and do it on your own time.
▶ Selling keeps you out there connecting with people.

Take a moment now and list some of the specific values that you find in selling, or that you would like to find:

▶ _____
▶ _____

You as a Seller

This area is uncomfortable for some people, but it is crucial that you dig down and find these answers. This is your chance to recognize and appreciate the unique strengths and qualities that you bring to selling. It isn't an ego trip. It's a tool you need in order to succeed at sales. What if Mother Teresa had said, "Oh, I'm no good at asking for money. Why would they give it to *me*?" With that attitude, she would never have contributed to the world as she did.

It helps to think about this question not in terms of *This is what's so great about me*, but in terms of *These are the skills I bring to the endeavor. My product is great and I'm representing it well because…*

Ask yourself these questions to tease out what you value about yourself as a seller:

▶ What do you bring to the table?
▶ What do you do well in sales?
▶ What is your favorite part of selling?
▶ What's the best experience you ever had selling?
▶ What qualities did you see in yourself at that time?
▶ What skills do you have that might be useful in selling?
▶ In what kinds of selling situations would you be particularly good?

People have answered:

▶ I genuinely like people, and they sense that.
▶ I'm someone who gets excited about things, and that makes it fun for me and for other people.
▶ I stick with things, and that's a big advantage in sales.
▶ I am my product's biggest fan, and like talking about it.

What are the specific values you see in yourself as a seller?

▶ _____
▶ _____

Your Product or Service

Everyone agrees that it's important to be clear on the value of your product or service, but Step #2 asks you to become clear in a very personal way. You can still talk about all the great benefits that everyone discusses, but find some values that are uniquely yours, and about which you can speak with personal conviction. Let yourself fall in love with your product or service, so that talking about it becomes a joy.

Here are some questions to get the juices flowing:

▶ What is your favorite thing about your product or service?
▶ What is the most personally valuable or meaningful thing about it for you?
▶ If you couldn't talk about any of the standard benefits, what would you say about it?
▶ What makes your product or service truly valuable to people?
▶ What are some of the things people get from using it?

Some answers people have given are:

▶ The insurance policy I sell really is the best value for people. They get the most benefits for the least amount of money.
▶ The artists I represent all use color in a way that just makes my heart sing.
▶ My mobile phones are, honest to God, the most fun. They have the best color, the most bells and whistles, and the most exciting games.
▶ I was born and raised in Chicago, and I love this town. Booking conventions and welcoming people to my city is like heaven for me.

What do you personally find most valuable about your product or service?

▶ _____

▶ _____

Your Buyers or Contacts

Your relationship with your contacts is the most important element of the Soul of Selling.

What you can, and cannot, control

"How do I know what people will be like?" Sally asked. "I have no way of knowing that." She's right. You have no way of knowing who you will encounter or how they will behave. And you certainly have no control over what kind of day they're having, or what they say to you. Most importantly, you can't control whether or not they buy. You can give them the best possible chance, and make it as easy as you can for them to buy—but in the end, it's their decision.

One thing you can control is the attitude you bring to your interaction with them. Another is your reaction to whatever they say or do. This is the power of the Soul of Selling. You decide *ahead of time*, before you even know their names, what your attitude toward them will be. The Soul of Selling asks you to create and hold a positive stance toward people, one that honors, appreciates and respects everyone with whom you speak—regardless of whether or not they buy, and regardless of how they speak or behave. This respect and appreciation is the lynchpin of the Soul of Selling. It is what guarantees integrity—and it is a big part of the ease.

"Yeah, but what if…"

People ask me, "No matter *what*?! What if they get really abusive, or come at you with a knife?" Obviously, if they get abusive and you no longer feel good about interacting with them, simply excuse yourself and respectfully end the conversation. If they come at you with a knife, run!

What are you willing to see?

Step #2 asks you to say what you are *willing* to see and appreciate in each of your contacts or buyers. To do this, you must be willing to look beyond the limitations of their personality or circumstances, and beyond how they may be feeling or behaving when they are with you, to some universal human values that we all share.

For instance, we all have the qualities of love, honesty, compassion and strength—to name a few. Sometimes these qualities are clouded by what's going on in our personalities. When we are anxious, depressed, angry, or uncertain, sometimes these qualities are not always very apparent. But they still exist, perhaps covered by layers of fear and defensiveness.

Your guarantee is to be willing to *see beyond whatever their mood or behavior may be, to the best in them.* You hold that vision of them, no matter what they do or say. This step will empower you beyond your wildest dreams.

When you don't make this guarantee to see the best in people, and determine ahead of time what that "best" is, anything can happen. If you talk with someone who is being cold and sullen, you could become defensive and withdraw. If someone is antagonistic, you could get reactive. But when you have *already decided* how you are going to be with them, then you are in charge. No matter what they do, you follow your game plan. You learn to look beyond your immediate emotional reaction to them, and hold to the high road for yourself and for them. (You are, after all, being the best in yourself in order to see the best in them.) This is what will keep you going when you want to stop, and help you go beyond where you have ever gone before.

Dan told me a great story about how this worked for him. He is a techie guy in his twenties who is working on his social and selling skills, but is still more comfortable with electronics. One day a young woman dragging a three-year-old struggled into the television section, where he was working that day. "In a nanosecond, I had her pegged," Dan said. "No money, an hour-and-a-half of my time with a screaming kid, and no sale. Either she was a single mom with no money, or she was just on a shopping excursion for her husband. I turned for the restroom, but my manager caught me and sent me over to her. As I was walking toward her, I remembered, *Oh yeah, I have to see her as a good person who loves people.*

"So I focused on that. The kid was a screamer, so it was hard. I had to keep refocusing and refocusing, seeing her as someone who loved people. I pictured her husband, but that didn't work, so I pictured her mom and how happy she must be to have a grandchild, even this kid. I pictured this woman as a loving mother, which I actually could see she was. I told her all about the HD models, and had her talk to the finance guy a bit while I went back to my desk and read from my Showcase Folder where I keep all this stuff about how I'm willing to see people.

"So then she's back, and she says she wants exactly the model we talked about. I kind of look up, because I'm expecting her to have all kinds of objections. But she's got it all worked out. She's cool. She buys.

"As she's leaving, she goes, 'Dan, I want to thank you for being so good to us, and so patient with Tommy.' I wasn't so sure about this stuff, but now I see how it works. I'll do it again."

Remember, you're being good to the other person—but you're being even better to yourself.

Here are some questions to start you thinking about what you are willing to value in your contacts:

▸ What are some universal positive traits that we all have, beneath it all?
▸ What are you willing to respect in everyone you encounter?
▸ What are you willing to honor in everyone you encounter?
▸ What are you willing to appreciate in everyone you encounter?
▸ What are the qualities you most admire in people?

▶ What are some things you like about yourself?

▶ Are you willing to see those qualities in other people?

▶ What good are you willing to see in people, no matter what they do or say?

And some answers:

▶ I know that everybody has aspirations in life to contribute. We all want to leave the world a better place than we found it.

▶ Everybody is doing the best they can, and wants to be as good as they can be.

▶ Everybody has a bottom-line integrity, whether or not they are real in touch with it.

▶ Everybody has a spark of love in them

What are some qualities that you are willing to respect, admire, or appreciate about the people with whom you have contact in sales?

▶ _____

▶ _____

Let Step #2 be your source of inspiration, replenishment and renewal—and use it for all it is worth.

EXERCISES

Do this exercise at least every month to keep your inspiration fresh and your values alive:

EXERCISE #1: Take out your lists of values in all four areas and read them over. Are there any that have gotten a little stale, that aren't so important to you anymore, or that have faded? Cross them off. You want this list always to be current, clean and compelling— with no fat or fading.

CHAPTER 7

Step #3:
Create Your Speaking Bank

What if you knew that every word you said about your product or service would be riveting? What if you could count on your presentation being as fresh as it was the day those brilliant words came to you for the first time? And what if you knew your words had been crafted for exactly this point in time, and exactly these circumstances?

That is the job of a Speaking Bank. "Teaching is more than the act of sharing information. It is the art of making information irresistible." I framed this anonymous quote, because the *same is true of selling*. Step #3 is about making your product or service irresistible.

In this chapter, we'll go step-by-step through developing your Speaking Bank, creating powerful sound bites, and delivering them in a way that ignites people's enthusiasm.

WHAT IS A SPEAKING BANK?

Your Speaking Bank acts like a treasure chest. You have an abundance of gold and jewels to show people. All you have to do is slowly open the lid, and let people see the sparkle. They lean in, and begin to see the true value, the things that will make a real difference in their lives. Then you pick up the jewels one by one, and hold them up to the light so people can see them more clearly.

In more prosaic terms, your Speaking Bank is a collection of clear, engaging talking points that give your contacts all the information they need in order to buy, and the inspiration to do so. Having these points at your fingertips gives you confidence. You know your message has been crafted to inform and inspire, and you can trust it to do its job. You can focus your attention on honoring and appreciating your contacts, rather than on figuring out what to say.

Does your Speaking Bank contain all the words that will ever pass between you and your contacts? No. It simply engages people. It draws them in so that they want to hear more. It opens the door to deeper, more specific talk about your product or service.

As you put together your Speaking Bank, you:

▸ *Gather* together all the information contacts need in order to make a good choice into pithy, persuasive sound bites
▸ *Galvanize* your contacts to want more
▸ *Gain* confidence about what you say and how you say it, so that you approach any situation positively and enthusiastically

THE SPEAKING BANK "YEAH, BUTS"

Whoa, Nellie!! Putting together information about the product?! And did I hear the word "speaking?!" When we come to this point in the seminar, people glaze over so thoroughly that it's as if we're in an underwater conference room. Everything seems to happen in slow motion. I can almost see the bubbles glubbing up. One man actually went to sleep and fell out of his chair onto the floor!

The purpose of Step #3 is to make talking about your product or service *easier* and *more inspiring*. But because it gets specific, and because it involves presentation, mental chatter often gets so agitated that it overwhelms itself and goes unconscious. So before we go any further, let's deal with some of that chatter and the Step #3 "Yeah, buts."

Yeah, but… #1: I can't write.

A blank piece of paper is some people's worst nightmare. The thought of filling it with pithy, salient features and benefits of their product or service makes them crazy, or hopeless. Take heart. You do not have to know anything about writing to create your Speaking Bank. You just need to answer some questions about your product or service. You need to fill in the blanks. The writing creates itself out of the exercises in this chapter.

Yeah, but... #2: I don't *wanna* write.

Newcomers to selling dread Step #3, but they are painfully in touch with the disadvantages of *not* having a Speaking Bank. One of the most common beginners' complaints is: "I don't know what to say, and I don't want to say the wrong thing." They are usually willing to go forward, because the imagined discomfort of creating a Speaking Bank is less than the real discomfort of not knowing what to say and feeling tongue-tied.

Veterans are a different story. Professional sellers sometimes figure they know what to say, and don't want to mess with a good thing. If it's not broken, why fix it? There's something to that. Check what you have. If it's not broken, you don't have to fix it. But if you check it, you will at least know that it's in good shape. And you may find a few little things you want to tweak or improve. Use this as an opportunity to fine-tune your message, and to break it up into sound bites for various situations.

Yeah, but... #3: I can't speak.

By now, most of us are aware of surveys showing that fear of public speaking consistently beats out fear of dying as people's greatest fear. Even if you don't find yourself behind a podium addressing 5,000 people about what you sell, delivering your presentation is a form of speaking. It can be uncomfortable.

Step #3 is designed to alleviate some of that discomfort. You'll know what you are going to say, and the guidelines in this chapter make delivering your Speaking Bank like saying hello to your best friend.

Yeah, but... #4: Did you say *practice*?

Yes. It's awful, I know—whether you do it in front of the mirror, in front of friends or colleagues, or (much more powerfully) on videotape. Here's the good news: When you have the courage to practice, you exhaust the nervousness. You make all the mistakes and call forth all the stage fright *before* you get in front of your contacts. By the time you actually deliver your presentation, you are cool, calm and confident. You've faced the demons, so speaking to your contacts is a walk in the park. It's like training with weights on your ankles, and then running the race without them.

"I'M BETTER IF I JUST WING IT!"

Only one person in a hundred is better off just winging it. Why take the chance that you are that one person, when your self-esteem and livelihood are on the line? I've seen people who are natural sellers, who do all the good work of Steps #1 and #2, and who nevertheless do not succeed because they haven't been systematic about putting together their presentation. They get into situations like these:

▸ "I love working with my clients, and I'm good at it," says Jean, a financial advisor. "But when I talk to people about what I do, I get tongue-tied. I don't want to come across pushy or conceited, so I say these watered-down things. I wouldn't sign up for something that blurry and vague. I'm not surprised that they don't."

▸ "I know my software backward and forward," Kent told me. "I'm not gonna give people a half-assed description of it, but they kind of fade out about two minutes into my explanation."

When you have done Step #3, worries about your message and delivering it are behind you. If you are like Jean, you never feel tongue-tied again. If you are like Kent, you find a way to do your product justice and capture people's attention.

WHAT YOUR SPEAKING BANK LOOKS LIKE

Your Speaking Bank looks like a page or two of writing—or about two minutes of speaking. It is a series of loosely woven statements that can be taken apart and put back together in several different ways to create just the right words, and just the right number of words, for any situation.

If you read your Speaking Bank straight through, it makes sense. One thought flows seamlessly to the next—but you would almost never speak it straight through unless you were making a formal presentation. Your Speaking Bank is usually delivered in bite-size pieces, within a conversation.

Later in this chapter, you will learn to create those bite-size pieces. First, you'll create the complete Bank.

THE SIX ELEMENTS OF YOUR SPEAKING BANK

Your Speaking Bank always includes at least these six elements:

1. The Large Vision

This opening statement paints a broad picture of what your product is and why it is terrific. It should be intriguing, and the value you mention should be very general. Give people a vision large enough to encompass many different interests, needs and desires—and let them discover for themselves where they fit in. Each person might see a different piece, but they can all imagine themselves involved in some way.

Here are some broad, intriguing one-sentence descriptions of large visions:

▶ Everyone in the family loves this car. (Mom might think, *It's easy to keep clean, and has lots of room for car-pooling.* Dad might think, *So it's not a chick car. I can take it to golf.* The kids might think, *Lots of room, windows, maybe a video monitor.* A single person with no children might think, *Ah, it's versatile.*)

▶ We make tax time easier. ("Easier" might mean "faster," or "I don't have to do as much research," or "They won't ask me as many questions," or "fewer forms," or even "They're nicer people.")

2. Features

Features are your product or service's specifications, qualities and characteristics. Plasma screen vs. regular screen. A word processing program vs. a spreadsheet program. A scanner/copier/printer vs. a dedicated scanner. Life coaching vs. financial coaching. Here are some feature statements:

▶ This vacation package is five days and four nights in a four-star Waikiki hotel, rental car included.

▶ We come to your house, measure and install the drapes within four days after you choose the fabric.

Telling people your product's features paints a picture in their minds—and this is essential. Unless they can see it in their mind's eye, they spend the rest of the conversation trying to picture what you're talking about—or tuning out because they can't key in to what you are saying. I learned this early on when I was selling seminars. I'd talk about the benefits, and the ways in which it had changed people's lives. Often the first question was, "How is it set up? Do you sit in a circle or at tables?" Those people probably hadn't heard much of what I said, because they were trying to get a picture of the seminar in their mind's eye.

When you talk about features, you are grounding your Larger Vision with specifics. "This is the printer of your dreams, and people are going to love seeing your stuff" is a great Larger Vision. It's intriguing and broad. But they probably don't yet have a picture in their minds. Is it laser or inkjet? Color or black and white? Is it also a fax, scanner, or copier? What is the footprint? Do you have a picture to show them, if you're not standing by the printer?

People are sometimes kind enough to draw this information out of you with questions if they have the interest and energy—but you can't count on your contacts to work that hard. Even if they are willing, you're not building their confidence in you.

3. Benefits

Features are what is *so* about your product or service. Benefits are what is *good* about it. What does your product or service do for people? What value do they get? What need does it fulfill? Why should people buy your product or service, rather than another one? What is unique about it?

Why, specifically, is your product or service "terrific," "fantastic," "the best," or whatever you said it was in your Large Vision? What's in it for them? Here are some descriptions of benefits:

▸ Even though this shirt looks and feels like silk, you can just wash it and stick it in the dryer.
▸ Our ski school uses video feedback so your muscles can actually "see" how to do it better.
▸ Our hookup is simple: You connect the blue line to the blue plug, the red line to the red plug, turn on the machine and you're set to go.
▸ We offer a money-back guarantee, no questions asked, if you return it within thirty days.

You'll want to include the standard benefits that everyone knows about, and also some of the personal benefits you discovered in Step #2.

4. Examples of the value

After you *tell* people about your product's benefits, *show* them. Give an example or two that demonstrate how your product or service helped people. Put it in the hands of real people with whom your contacts can identify, and let them show it off. Bring the story to life. Show people how it filled a need or expanded people's lives:

▶ My neighbor bought this model lawnmower and now spends two-thirds of the time he used to spend on his yard. He even brought me a bottle of wine to thank me.
▶ One of our clients just asked us to check over her tax return, and we saved her $876.
▶ After Unified consulted with us for a year, their productivity was up 17%.

5. Applications

Certain products and services can be used in several ways. If yours is one of these, tell people about it. (Don't try this with the lawnmower!)

▶ Our service offers both individual coaching for executives and training for managers.
▶ This PDA can do email, and then become a game station.
▶ When you master this small business financial software, you can use it for your personal finances as well.

6. Cost

You may not talk about cost until late in your conversation, but you need to include it in your Speaking Bank. You and your contact both need to know whether or not they can afford it, or if they are even in the ballgame. Where you place the cost within the conversation depends on many variables. Unless the cost itself is the primary selling point, you usually want to line up the vision, features, benefits and examples—and also get a sense of where your contact is—before you go to the cost.

It's especially important to talk about the cost when you practice your Speaking Bank. Even veteran sellers who say they don't have trouble talking about cost are sometimes stunned to watch themselves on video—crossing their arms, squirming, or in some other way suggesting their discomfort. To speak with grace and ease about cost, be sure you are clear in your own mind that it is fair. Then just give people the amount without hedging, hiding, justifying, or rationalizing. Take a stand for the value of what you are offering.

▶ The fee for editing this book is $20,000, payable half when I start, and half after I finish.

▶ Your investment for one consulting session is $200.

▶ The cost of the seminar is $950.

TWO SAMPLE SPEAKING BANKS

Here are two sample Speaking Banks, one for a product and the other for a service. The first is for a cordless phone. The second is for the Soul of Selling Seminar.

Cordless Phone

This phone is our most practical and flexible model. (*The Large Vision*: People immediately begin to think what would make it practical and flexible for them. They are beginning to sort out what their piece of the vision is. "Practical" might mean sturdy, or that it can be hung on a wall, or that it doesn't have so many features that they get confused.)

It's a cordless 2.4 GHz digital phone and answering system, black, one-line with caller ID. (*Features*: You get a picture in your mind.)

The voice quality is clear and the menu is so easy that most people don't even need the manual to set it up. It's one of only two models we have that comes with its own headset. This is our least returned brand, so you shouldn't have any problem with it—but there's a one-year warrantee and a thirty-day return policy if you don't like it for any reason. (*Benefits*: What makes it uniquely attractive and what might be in it for them.)

I personally like that it's shock- and water-resistant. I'm not just talking about the kids. I've spilled coffee all over my desk more times than you can imagine. The other things I like about it are that it has a backlit display so it's easy to see. You can also see the caller ID more easily because it fits upright in the stand rather than lying down in the cradle like other models. With those models, I always had to stand up to see who was calling, because they were flat on the desk. The other thing I like is that the stand is compact, so it has a small footprint. And it's stylish. I think it looks great. (*Your personal value*: These are benefits to which you can speak with personal conviction. You're conveying information, and also establishing a personal relationship with your contact.)

A woman came into the store last week to buy a CD player, and she stopped here on her way out to tell me how much she loves this phone, which she bought a month ago. She works at home as a tech writer. She loves the voice quality, and said people had actually commented on it.

That's only the third time I've been working here that someone's done that. She thinks this is the world's best phone. (*Example* of the value, a benefit someone got.)

It's expandable to four handsets so it's great for a home office, or a home that might become an office. (*Applications*: The uses that are different from the one you assume.)

And it's only $_____. (*Cost*)

The Soul of Selling Seminar

What if you could guarantee the exact sales results you wanted, every time? What if you were also confident in being a person of honor and integrity, knowing that everyone you contacted was respected, honored and appreciated—whether or not they bought your product or service? And what if you knew how to recharge your passion at will, and to sell with ease? That is the Fourfold Guarantee of the Soul of Selling: Results, Integrity, Passion and Ease—every time. (*The Large Vision*. If this sounds familiar to you, it is the Vision that opened this book.)

This one-day seminar gives your people six steps that lead them gently but inevitably to exactly those guarantees. They deliver precisely the sales results they promise. They also feel great about themselves because everyone with whom they speak is in better shape after the conversation than they were before it. We use powerful exercises and coaching to help your group individualize each of the six steps to their own specific situation. The seminar comes with a workbook that people can use over and over to refresh their enthusiasm. (*Features*)

Our clients report that whatever their results had been before the seminar, they got even better. They sold more, in less time, with less effort and less burnout. They learned to see selling as service, and had a technology for repeating their success. They actually began to enjoy selling. The Soul of Selling takes the guesswork out of results, and the sleaze out of sales. You win big, and sell with honor. (*Benefits*)

People tell me I was born to do this, and I love it more than anything. (*Personal Value*)

One large auto dealer in the San Francisco Bay Area hired me to train their sales staff. In six months, their sales increased 12%. That was great, but my favorite part was when the owner, who was a tough older guy, took me out to lunch. He asked, "What did you do to these people? They're happier. I don't know if that's good, but I like the numbers." (*Example of the value.*)

I can present a shorter version of this material in three to four hours, or partner with you in a longer program that produces exponential results. (*Applications*)

The fee for the one-day seminar is $_____ with a $45 materials fee. We can adjust that if you prefer the shorter or longer versions of the course. (*Cost*)

I have never actually spoken this Bank all the way through, although I've memorized it word for word. When I'm asked to speak for two minutes on the seminar (which is about the length of the above), I may not say it exactly this way—but I'll probably include all of this information.

I also have some "next level down" conversations in which I talk about clearing away negative thinking in the four areas, using promises as truing mechanisms, or the Honoring Sales Conversation. But by that time, the Speaking Bank information would be safely in my contact's hands, and our connection would be golden.

Now let's create your Speaking Bank.

CREATING YOUR SPEAKING BANK—THE EASY WAY

Creating your Speaking Bank can be easy and fun. Start by simply answering the questions below. Include all the important information, but remember that the Speaking Bank's purpose is simply to draw people in and intrigue them. You don't have to tell them everything here. You'll have plenty of time once you've won them over. For now, try to be enthusiastic but concise. Pack all that energy into as few words as possible.

When you're finished, we'll put all these answers together:

The Large Vision (2-4 sentences):

1. What does your product or service do for everybody? Each person may find his or her own benefit, but here we are looking for the common denominators.

_____

_____

Features (2-3 sentences)

2. What are the specifications or characteristics of your product or service that people need to know to get a picture of it in their minds?

_____

_____

Benefits (about 4 sentences)

3. What are the primary benefits or values of using your product or service?
4. What needs will it fulfill?
5. What makes it unique?
6. Why should people buy from you, rather than from someone else?

Your personal values (about 2 sentences)

7. What do you find uniquely, personally valuable about it? (You may want to refer to your answers in Step #2.)

Examples of its value (about 3 sentences)

8. What is one good example of the value someone got from using your product or service?

Applications (about 2 sentences, if necessary)

9. If there are any other ways your product or service can be used, what are they?

Cost (1 sentence)

10. What is the cost of your product or service, expressed as a fee or investment?

BRING YOUR SPEAKING BANK TOGETHER

Take a moment now to bring all your answers together and create your own Speaking Bank. Just write one answer after the other. You can then edit your work, if you like, to make it flow more smoothly.

ɔu edit your Bank, try this method: Imagine that your prime con-
̲̲̲, ̲he person you most want to buy from you, says, "You have two
minutes to tell me about your product. I won't interrupt you. At the end
of two minutes, I'll tell you whether or not I'm buying." Write down
what you would say.

Congratulations! You have a Speaking Bank. Now, what do you do
with it?

PUTTING YOUR SPEAKING BANK TO WORK

Remember, your Speaking Bank is like a treasure chest of words. It's
always with you, and you can pull from it whatever you need. For instance, the person selling the digital phone in the first sample Speaking
Bank would never just speak that Bank all the way through. She would
connect with her contact, find out what the contact was looking for,
and pull from the Speaking Bank to meet those needs. Depending on
what the customer wanted, she might emphasize the excellent digital
voice quality, the small footprint and stylishness, or the ease of use.
She might say everything that was in the Speaking Bank, but do so in
one, two, or three-sentence sound bites as the information fit into their
conversation.

The difference between conducting this conversation with a Speaking Bank in the back of your mind, and without one, is that the Speaking Bank puts the very best information at your fingertips. You don't
have to stop and think about what to say. The words take care of themselves, and you can give all your energy to your contact. It's like having
a well-stocked kitchen before undertaking a major cooking project. If
you need marjoram, it's in the spice rack. If you need whole-wheat flour,
it's in the pantry. You don't have to stop and run out to the store every
five minutes. Everything is convenient, just waiting to be picked up and
used.

BITE-SIZE PIECES: MAKE IT EASY TO SWALLOW

Once you have your Speaking Bank, the next step is to create some
bite-size pieces. These one- or two-sentence sound bites give you tre-
mendous flexibility, and the power to intrigue people very quickly. Say
you are at a party, and the man next to you asks, "What do you do?"
You have several options, and having a great sound bite gives you one
that works! You don't have to choose between "I sell cordless phones,"

which has about as much punch as saying "I feed my dog every morning," and a five-minute speech about the phones in your department, GHz, MHz and digital whatsits.

Instead, you can say, "I sell phones that make the old way of calling obsolete. People get a big kick out of using them." You give him your first sound bite, and then see if he wants to hear more. If he doesn't, talk about the canapés. If he does, give him the next piece.

How do you know which piece to choose next? If he indicates an interest in some aspect of your phones, like "big kick," then go there. Tell him what is fun about your phone. Why do people get a kick out of it? Color? Elegance? Footprint? If he shows an interest in something else, talk about that. If he keeps responding positively and the two of you are connected, you can tell him more—or at least ask if he would really like to hear more—without imposing on him or being pushy.

These sound bites are invaluable when you don't know how much time or attention the other person is prepared to give you. This is their great advantage over "elevator speeches"—the traditional business response to "What do you do?" Elevator speeches usually take at least twenty to thirty seconds. This is too long. Pay attention as the second hand on your watch counts off twenty to thirty seconds. Then ask yourself how you would respond to an answer that long if you had just asked someone casually what they did, and weren't really interested in their response.

What every reporter knows

You need to get people their information quickly. Newspaper editors have always known how to do this. Reporters are taught to put all the important information in the first sentence, or the (very short) first paragraph, of the story. They assume that this one paragraph is all people will read. That means they only have those one or two sentences to get across all the crucial information. If those sentences are intriguing enough to catch readers' attention, they may go on to the second, third or fourth paragraphs. Each paragraph fleshes out a few more details, but reporters always assume that people will *not* read on unless they have a good reason to do so.

It might look like this:

> Bill Smith set the all-time sales record for Acme Industries this year with $4 million, scoring a repeat victory. (*This is all the crucial information.*)

Smith beat his own record of $3.7 million, set last year. Second and third places went to Jane Doe ($3.2 million) and Jose Mendoza ($2.9 million), who were also honored at the Awards Luncheon at the Centennial Hotel on Thursday. (Fleshing out the story and adding information)

"I owe it all to the Soul of Selling," Smith said. (*More information and further fleshing out.*)

Opening sound bites

The newspaper story is an excellent guide for creating bite-size pieces from your Speaking Bank. You start with a hook, a point of interest and intrigue, and give a broad statement of your message. Let's take the example from the party: "I sell phones that make the old way of calling obsolete. People get a big kick out of using them." What do we know from this? We know that you sell phones, not cars. We know that those phones are somehow innovative, on the cutting edge. We don't know where that edge lies, however, and we have a feeling we might miss something if we don't find out. We also know that these phones are fun. But again, we don't know exactly why. That's intriguing.

In your first ten-second sound bite, you want two things:

1. The basic, essential information (innovative phones, not cars)
2. A "hook" that intrigues people and leaves them wanting to know more

Pretend you have only ten seconds to capture someone's interest, and to give them a sense of what you're selling and why it is valuable. Assume that this is all you will ever say to the person. After you have your first sound bite, you can create four to five more ten-second sound bites that "flesh out" the story as the paragraphs of a newspaper story would—giving additional information, personalizing what you are saying and keeping the listener intrigued.

I like to have separate opening sound bites for business and social occasions. Both require information and relationship building. In business, the focus is on information. For social situations, I focus on relationship building and see whether it morphs into a business conversation. Here is how it might sound for both the phone and the Soul of Selling Seminar.

BUSINESS:

▶ This is your answer if you want a 2.4 GHz digital cordless phone with an answering system. It's stylish, expandable, easy to operate, and top quality by the leading manufacturer.

▶ The Soul of Selling guarantees that you'll sell exactly as much as you promise, and also honor everyone with whom you speak. It takes the guesswork out of results and the stress out of selling.

SOCIAL:

▶ I sell the best phone I've ever used. It makes everything fun and easy.

▶ I give a seminar that's the joy of my life. You learn to guarantee your sales results, every time, and also guarantee that everyone you talk to is respected and appreciated—whether or not they buy.

Keep an eye on how people are responding as you speak. If you sense they are sorry they asked, stop. If people are not intrigued by these ten-second sound bites, then the phone or the seminar probably are not for them. No problem. Enjoy the party, or get on to the next contact. If they are still interested and attentive, keep going. Try your next ten-second sound bite.

Your opening ten-second sound bite

To create your opening ten-second sound bite, consider the minimal information that people need in order to make sense of what you're talking about (it's a *phone!*), and something you can say to intrigue or interest them. Write it here, or in your notebook.

Your family of ten-second sound bites

Now that you have given all the essential information and gotten their attention, you can start fleshing out the story. Tell them more about what you offer, but remember to keep their attention. In this space or your notebook, create two more ten-second sound bites about your product or service:

Your opening twenty-second sound bite

You may also want to create a ten-second opening sound bite for occasions when you know you will have at least twenty seconds of people's attention. Your twenty-second sound bite may include, and then build on, what you say in your ten-second opening sound bite. You can create both business and social twenty-second sound bites, but situations where you know you have twenty seconds are usually business-oriented. These might include:

▶ Introductions around the table at professional gatherings, when everyone is asked to say their name and what they do
▶ Introductions to short talks
▶ When you have been introduced to someone specifically because of what you offer, and either they or the person who introduced you has indicated that they are interested in hearing more than ten seconds

If you have unspoken permission for twenty seconds in a social situation, you're usually safe in gearing what you say to business. Here are twenty-second sound bites for the phone and seminar:

▶ It's our most practical and flexible cordless phone system, and our most popular. The voice quality is superb and people find it easy to use. It's one line with caller ID, its own headset, and up to four handsets. It looks great on a desk, and I like the small footprint. It's a great deal at $99.95. People love it.
▶ This seminar gives you six simple, powerful steps that lead you inevitably to the sales numbers of your choice, and also guide you through conversations that honor, respect and appreciate everyone with whom you speak—whether or not they buy. You get more sales, in less time with less stress, and you also get a technology for repeating your success. You sell with honor, and companies have increased their numbers as much as 23%.

Take a minute to create your twenty-second sound bite:

_____

_____

Stay flexible with your Speaking Bank and sound bites. Every product or service is different, and every seller has slightly different needs. You may need a five-second sound bite, or a thirty- or forty-five-second sound bite. As you go forward, be alert to what works best for you.

Make sure you have everything you need at your fingertips when you go out to sell.

Tools like the Speaking Bank and the sound bites are essential, but *how* you speak to people is as important as what you say.

ARE YOU TALKIN' TO *ME?*

Most of us have had the experience of liking a product and being almost ready to buy—except that something is just a little "off" with the person selling it. You may not be able to put your finger on what it is, but something is out of sync. You just don't feel comfortable buying from them. I've actually left a store, and returned later to buy the same product from someone else.

What is that about? Usually, we feel that something is just a little "off" because it *is* a little "off." The person may have some doubt about what they are selling, or about themselves, or about selling in general, or about *us!* Or they may just be having a bad day. Or something is going on in their life that they are bringing into the selling process, like a death or divorce. Whatever it is, something is keeping them from being 100% present with you, focused on supporting you in making a good choice about their product or service. It may not be in anything they say. It usually isn't. It's more often in their presence, their tone of voice, or their body language.

When you love your product or service, people pick up these same kinds of nonverbal clues. People feel it when you genuinely love selling as a way to serve and support people. They feel terrific when you are seeing the best in them, whether or not they even know that's what you are doing! This kind of positive experience may not be the deciding factor in whether or not they buy, but it can definitely influence the outcome. It never hurts, and it can help. Minimally, you feel good about what you are doing and how you are doing it.

People listen to your demeanor, delivery and presence as much as they listen to your words. If you and another person are offering exactly the same thing, and everything else is equal, the question becomes whether they would rather buy from you, or from the other person.

EIGHT SECRETS OF A GREAT PRESENTATION

How do you deliver your message so that people want to hear more? Here are eight tools for presenting your Speaking Bank in the most effective way:

1. Focus your attention on the other person.

We start out with the best of intentions, determined to make the other person feel like the center of the universe. We want to serve and support. But as night follows day, the attention inevitably drifts back to us. Fred told me, "I do well, but then I find myself asking, *How am I doing? Am I doing it right? Where am I in the Speaking Bank? What should I say next? What does he or she think of me?*"

If this happens to you, gently but firmly take your attention and place it back on the other person. In a sense, talking with your contact is like meditation. When you meditate, you empty your mind—but thoughts always return. When they do, you don't make a big deal out of it. You just watch the thought, let it go, and return to the object of your meditation. Do the same thing here. Watch the thoughts, let them go, and return to your contact.

Keeping your attention on the other person is actually a way to make yourself more comfortable. When you are focused on serving them, you don't ask self-referential questions like *How am I doing?* The best cure for stage fright, or any kind of performance anxiety, is to focus your attention on someone else. Concentrate on contributing to them, and you forget to worry about how you are doing.

2. Listen to them with your eyes.

Listen not just to what your contacts are saying, but also to their body language, facial expressions and energy. Feel into where they are. Are their arms crossed? It doesn't necessarily mean that they are saying "No," but they may feel a little protective or uncomfortable. Tread softly for a while. Are they frowning? Again, it may not be a bad sign—but notice it, and keep aware that it *might* be. Are they looking at you? If they're not with you, where are they? When you are aware of how they are responding, you are in a position to make course corrections.

3. Call forth your own enthusiasm.

Let the experience of what you love about your product or service live within you, and speak from that place of inspiration. People pick up on it, and this is what they take away with them.

4. Learn to pat your head and rub your stomach.

Wait! Should you be listening to them with your eyes, or living in your own enthusiasm? Both! Pat your head and rub your stomach. Think back to the first time someone asked you to try this parlor trick. Remember how little time it took you to go from total fumbling, to mastery? Do the same thing here. You'll have it within five minutes. Let your passion live within you, at the same time that you focus all your attention on the other person. If you are truly excited about your product or service, it's easy to let that be present in you. If you are really interested in the other person, that's easy as well. You are balancing two easy, enjoyable things.

5. Make course corrections.

When you ride a bike, you are almost never balanced perfectly. You're constantly making tiny corrections that keep you and the bike moving forward. The same is true of selling. You are alert to people's reactions, and sensitive to whether they need you to step forward a little, or step back. If the other person gets very quiet, for instance, you might stop talking about the benefits for a moment and ask them more about their needs.

Another way to modulate the conversation is in your tone of voice and style. Extreme introverts are sometimes uncomfortable if you're figuratively jumping up and down on a table with a lampshade on your head. For their sakes, speak more quietly, or more slowly. You can be enthusiastic without overpowering them. Match your level of expression or enthusiasm to where they are. On the other hand, if you are an introvert and your contact is the extrovert, you may need to bring yourself forward a bit.

Have you ever introduced two friends, hoping they would hit it off? You watch their interaction, sometimes jumping in with information that will smooth a rough spot, sometimes just being quiet and letting them discover one another. When you introduce your contact and your product, you make these same kinds of course corrections. Your friends don't always hit it off, and not everybody buys. All you are doing is providing a fertile ground for the relationship. You can't make the seed grow, but you can give it the best chance for success.

6. Do what works for them, not what works for you.

Remember, it's your contacts' show, not yours. They are the stars, and the attention is on them. If they don't move as quickly as you do mentally, slow down. If they want to move more quickly, speed up. Stay centered in yourself and serve your product well, but make the *style* of your presentation work for your contact—whether or not that style is your first choice.

You don't have to be exactly *like* your contact, but you need to be with that person in a way that is comfortable for him or her. Be flexible enough to talk to anyone, under any circumstances. I had to learn, for instance, that a soft, slow presentation can be just as effective—in many cases, more so—than my naturally effusive style.

7. When in doubt, tell the truth.

Sometimes conversations just become baffling, in sales and in life. You can't for the life of you figure out what's going on with your contact, what they're thinking, or what they need. When I'm baffled, I've found the best thing to do is tell the truth. If I ask a question or two and get monosyllabic answers, and I can't see any other clues, I might ask, "Is this of interest to you?" or "Is this making any sense?" Of course, you have to be prepared for honest answers if you ask these kinds of questions. Honesty is, after all, what you really want. If they're not interested, you're wasting your time and theirs. Better to have a smile, a handshake, a "thank you" and a good-bye. If you're not boring them, you have at least interrupted the baffling energy and can start anew, perhaps down a different path.

As a last resort, I pretend that I can say whatever I want, which leads to the ultimate secret of a great presentation…

8. It's just us chickens.

When you don't know what else to do, imagine what you might do if the person sitting across from you, or on the other end of the phone, were a good friend. Forget about how you "should" act, and be yourself. People appreciate authenticity more than you can imagine. When you are real, it gives them permission to be real.

Some of my best moments in selling have come when I took off my seller hat and said something like, "You know, I feel very strange. It doesn't seem like I'm giving you what you need, and I can't figure out what that is. Can you help me out? Is what we're doing here working for you?" Then whatever they tell you, you simply take them at their word.

GETTING TO CARNEGIE HALL

We've all heard the story about the tourist who stops a New Yorker to ask, "How do you get to Carnegie Hall?"

The answer, of course, is, "Practice, practice, practice."

In the midst of meeting and connecting with your customers, making sure they have all the information they need, staying alert to their reactions, making course corrections, and...oh, yes...being yourself, the last thing you need is to be trying to remember what's in your Speaking Bank and how best to present it.

I'm going to suggest you do two things that you already know are good ideas:

▸ *Memorize* your Speaking Bank.
▸ *Practice* it. Say it in the mirror. Speak your whole Bank, all the way through. Yes, it's an artificial situation. All the better. When you get to the more natural situation with another person, it will be that much easier. Or better yet, videotape it and *watch the playback*. This is the most powerful tool I know for presentation training. You will see things you don't even know you're seeing, and correct them without even thinking about it. People who are courageous enough to practice on video improve their presentations exponentially, and experience much more ease and comfort when they actually deliver their message.

Memorizing and practicing can be uncomfortable, but it's better to be uncomfortable in private. There's nobody watching, and you aren't putting your results at risk.

THE BOTTOM LINE: HAVING FUN

There are many, many guidelines in this chapter. The bottom line is this: Be clear what you want to say about your product or service and its value. Bring all the enthusiasm you have to the table, then connect with the other person and speak to where they are. Throughout it all, have fun. That's all you really need to remember.

EXERCISES

EXERCISE #1: Create your Speaking Bank, if you have not already done so. Mark your calendar to revise it in a month.

EXERCISE #2: Speak your Speaking Bank into the mirror, to a friend and/or into a video camera. You might never actually speak it this way in "real life," but watching the tape or getting feedback from your friend will teach you things you can't learn any other way.

CHAPTER 8

Step #4: Promise Your Result

"I thought I did better without promises, that they just made me anxious," Ellen told me. "Now I love them because they keep me steady. I'd be anxious *without* them!"

Step #4 is about learning to make a new kind of promise, and about making your word golden. The Soul of Selling promises are:

▸ *Crafted so that you win*, every time. They work for you, rather than against you.
▸ *Truing mechanisms* that bring support, direction and strength—not stress, grief and threats
▸ *Guarantees for success* that keep you on track, moving forward in exactly the direction you want to go

WHAT IS A PROMISE?

When you promise something, you guarantee that it will happen. You say that you will do whatever is necessary to produce that particular result. If you aren't willing to guarantee it, you don't make the promise. In this chapter, you will learn the five qualities that a promise needs to have in order for you to keep it with ease, every time.

Remember, a promise is different from a goal. You work *toward* a goal, but you may or may not achieve it. Goals are often little more than hopes or wishes. A promise is your word, your guarantee. You stand behind it. It will happen—no matter what. (We're not throwing common sense out the window. If emergencies like deaths of loved ones or serious illness occur, you will make good on the promise at a later date.) It's a great way to live, and a great way to succeed in sales.

It goes without saying that when you reach Step #4, mental chatter goes wild. Promises involve both *getting specific* and *change*—mental chatter's two least favorite things. In mental chatter's world, to make a promise for *specific change* is to invite disaster! You are drawing a line in the sand when you make these kinds of promises:

▸ I will have three new clients by September 15.
▸ I will sell $400,000 by June 30.
▸ I will have twenty volunteers to clean up the park by next Friday.
▸ I will have sixty people at that fundraiser on October 7.

This can be a panicky, desperate time for mental chatter. It is apt to say things like, *I can't guarantee that stuff. I'd be lying if I did, because what if we're blown up? What if the house falls down and I have to save people? What about that? Huh? Do you see why I can't make any promises?* By now, you have some good tools for dealing with this kind of complaint. Note it, nod to it, and switch channels.

YEAH, BUT... "NO MATTER WHAT?"

"No matter what" is what gives your promise teeth. Without "no matter what," your promise is just a hope, a wish, or a vague direction in which to travel.

Yeah, but how can you do that without pressuring people to buy? mental chatter whines. *How can you guarantee what other people are going to do?* As usual, most of mental chatter's objections start with, "Yeah, but...":

▸ Yeah, but what if nobody is in the mood to buy that week? I can't help that, can I?
▸ Yeah, but my mother is sick and I might have to go to Houston.
▸ Yeah, but my kids come first and they might need me.
▸ Yeah, but what if I get sick?
▸ Yeah, but my daughter is graduating this spring.
▸ Yeah, but making the promise will make me crazy, and I won't be able to relax with people. Then I won't be able to appreciate and respect those people who aren't buying. And you said we had to do that, right? Are you telling me to go against my own ethics, and what you say?

The "yeah, buts" often have a defensive, whiney quality. And they often concern events and conditions that "might" happen. There's no "might" about it. These things *will* happen. Count on it! In the unlikely event that these things don't happen, you will not believe the importance that alphabetizing your spice rack or dusting your bookcases takes on. It will become life or death.

Some people think that in order to keep a promise, life has to stop. Life never stops, and that's why they have trouble keeping promises. You need to plan for life to continue, even when you're selling. Here are three good ways to keep life from getting in the way of keeping your promise:

▸ *Make arrangements for the expected.* Get the support you need to handle the kids *and* keep the promise. Figure out the graduation party now, months ahead of time. Don't leave things until the last minute. Those are the things that get in the way.

▸ *Expect the unexpected.* Know that wild events will intrude on exactly the time you planned to spend selling.

▸ *Start early, and keep going.* When you work ahead of schedule, you have room for life and for emergencies. When you put off selling until the last minute, you don't.

THE PROMISE OF PROMISES: WHAT THEY CAN DO FOR YOU

Why bother to make promises? Why expose yourself to that discomfort? Aren't they really just a way to manipulate yourself? No. *Promises are a covenant with yourself, and with your own potential in the world.* Whatever that means to you—money, prestige, personal growth, service to your family or community, or some combination of all these things—promises are your gateway to bringing more of yourself forward into the world, and to acting in more powerful and compassionate ways.

Making friends with promises is one of the most empowering things you can do. Promises give you five crucial benefits:

1. Promises move you forward.

Promises are how we move forward in life. They draw us toward what we want, and help us achieve it. I think of it as fishing for success. Imagine that you are standing at one end of a large room, and your ultimate goal is to get to the other end of the room. Now imagine that you have a small fishing rod, and that you cast out about fifteen feet. The hook goes into the floor, and you reel yourself up to the point where the hook went in. That's what happens when you keep the promise.

Then what? You cast out again, maybe eighteen feet this time. The hook goes into the floor and, again, you reel yourself in. Another promise kept. Each time you make and keep a promise, you are closer to where you want to be. You move toward your ultimate desire, the other end of the room, one promise at a time. You reel yourself into your own success.

2. Promises are your power.

When you keep your promises, no matter what, your word becomes like gravity. You can trust yourself, and other people can trust you. You know that when you promise something, you will deliver. Others know it, too. You have integrity, and that feels great. Being a person who keeps promises generates respect in a way that almost nothing else can. That's good for business, and even better for self-esteem.

3. Promises give you a sense of accomplishment.

When you promise a result, you create a challenge. When you meet that challenge, you know you have accomplished something.

Bob hated the whole idea of promises when we first spoke. "I'm not a kid," he said. "I do my best. That's enough. I work just as hard as I would if I had a promise." I told him that working hard wasn't the point. Results are the point. I invited him to try something.

"Try thinking of promises as an opportunity, as a secret strategy you got from a mentor," I said. "Let them take you to a whole new level. You don't even have to tell anybody you're making them. Try it for a month, give it a good shot, and see if there's a difference in your results. If there isn't, forget about making promises."

Bob agreed. His results improved, but that wasn't the best part. "I feel more productive," he said. "It's more fun to get the result when I've said I would do something, put myself up against it and won! I wouldn't go without making promises now." As I was leaving his office, his screen saver came on and I saw the word "Promise" floating and turning in space.

4. Promises help you relax.

In an odd way, promises actually remove stress. I used promises this way when I stopped smoking. I was not one of those people who wake up one day with the sniffles and say, "Hey, I don't think I'll smoke anymore." And they don't. I was horribly addicted, and stopping smoking was one of the hardest things I've ever done. The one advantage I had was that I understood the nature of promises from my life in sales. I knew better than to promise something I wasn't going to deliver, no matter what. I realized that if I ever stopped smoking, and then started again, I would never trust myself to quit.

So I waited until I was really, really ready and then set a "quit date." I haven't had a cigarette since then, because after the "quit date" I no longer gave myself the option of asking, *Well, should I or should I not have a cigarette?* I knew that if I kept that question open, if I waited to see whether or not I would have a cigarette, it was only a matter of time before I lit up.

I'm not saying it was easy. I chewed a lot of gum and took a lot of walks around the block. But I'd already answered the worst question: *Will I have a cigarette, or not?* The only question left was, *How can I deal with the discomfort of not smoking?* It was a lot easier to come up with solutions like fancy coffees, chewing gum, calling a friend, or playing with the cat than it was to engage the "To smoke or not to smoke" question—and I felt a lot better about myself.

Will I have a cigarette, or not? was a question heading in one direction—toward the cigarette. I might have had to ask that question forty times, but sooner or later the answer was going to be *Yes.*

Will I keep my selling promise, or will I give up and find an excuse because I can't stand the discomfort? is a question that's also headed in one direction. Sooner or later, the answer is going to be giving up. When you make a promise you are willing to keep, no matter what, the question shifts from *Will I keep my promise, or not?* to *What do I need to do to keep my promise?* In the end, strange as it may seem at first, that's a far more comfortable question.

5. Promises are a truing mechanism.

If it's two days before your promise is due and you aren't close to the result, you know it's time to change tactics. Promises tell you when you need a course correction.

6. Promises teach you to take a stand for your vision.

You learn what it is to take a stand for a product, service, project, or vision, and to bring it from the realm of ideas into reality and success. Talk is cheap, and so are good thoughts. Results matter. They make a difference in people's lives, in the world, and in your own life. It's great to think good thoughts—but if you want to have a serious impact, you also need to be skilled at getting results.

THE SOUL OF SELLING PROMISES: THE FIVE ESSENTIAL ELEMENTS

Crafting a good promise is the foundation for keeping it. If you craft your promise well, the rest is easy. The Soul of Selling promises contain five essential elements that make them work. When you include all five elements, your promise becomes a beacon that is easy to keep in sight.

The five essential elements of a Soul of Selling promise are:

1. Authentic

The promise is yours, not something forced on you from outside. You create it, you are the source of its energy, and you own it.

What if you have quotas imposed on you from outside? First, look to see if you can own them and make them your own. If you can do that, great. If you can't, talk to the person who assigns them to you. Try to negotiate something you can truly get behind. Your boss may be smart enough to know that you are more likely to keep a promise that you own.

"They made me do it" and "I didn't really want to promise that much" have no place in the Soul of Selling. If you can't own it, then it's not a Soul of Selling promise. Make only promises you can embrace, love and use to make your life sing.

2. Doable

Be realistic. Don't promise the impossible. It's better to promise less and deliver more, than to promise more and deliver less. Set yourself up to win. Start small, and build the habit of success. Stretch a little only after you've established a track record. Don't worry about promising too little—especially at first. When you have won with smaller promises, you can start making bigger ones. Limit your promises to what you are willing to do, no matter what.

3. For sales results, not for effort

Promising to call for three hours means nothing. Promising to call thirty people means nothing. Promising to make three sales means everything. This may sound harsh, but it's a fact of life in sales: *Trying doesn't count.*

When people are new to sales, they want to promise effort. "I'll make fifteen calls" or "I'll talk to five people." Making calls and talking to people are necessary, but not sufficient. You have to do them, but *just* doing them doesn't pay the rent. They don't keep your business open or earn commissions. Sales do that. Promising effort is like wanting orange juice and saying, "I'll climb four orange trees." Great. But what about the juice? Promising to have lunch with three people this week is effort. Promising to sell $50,000 this week is results.

Similarly, people sometimes want to promise brochure writing, making lists of people to call, or getting business cards. These are important, but ancillary activities. You'll do these things, and you may even promise to do them—but they are not part of your Step #4 promise for results.

Effort may be needed to produce the result, but promising effort gets you exactly that—effort. You're not out to work hard; you're out to get results. That may mean working hard, but the work is not the point. Results are the point.

4. For specific numbers

Make your promise for a specific number:

- ▶ Three new clients
- ▶ $50,000
- ▶ Four travel packages
- ▶ Two properties

Without a specific number in your promise, you have no idea where you are, or whether or not you've gotten where you were going. The specific number is the piece of concrete reality against which you measure your success. You have kept your promise when you've gotten three new clients, or sold $50,000, four travel packages, or two properties.

5. Defined by dates

Again, you need this piece of concrete reality against which to measure your success. By when will you produce the result? Without a due date, the promise has no teeth. If you promise to have three new clients, but don't say by when, the promise just hangs out there in space. It can't help or support you, because it's not grounded. Years could go by, and you would have no clients. And as time passes with no clarity about where you are with your promise, your energy hangs out there in space with your promise. Promises without due dates bleed off your energy without delivering a result.

Assigning a date to your promise gives it power. You have something to bump up against. You have a solid surface into which to cast out your fishing hook.

Your Soul of Selling promise must have all five of these elements. If one is missing, it's not a Soul of Selling promise. Here are some promises that incorporate all five elements:

- ▶ I will have six new clients by June 30.
- ▶ I will sell $600,000 of product by March 31.
- ▶ I will have forty people in the seminar by September 15.
- ▶ I will sell six cars by December 1.

CRAFTING YOUR PROMISE: THE NUTS AND BOLTS

Here's how it works: Fran wanted to craft a promise for her online art store. She approached the process with great enthusiasm, and started with: "I'll double in July what I did in June!!"

I applauded her eagerness, and asked her how much she made in June. She didn't know. Already, we were in trouble. She wasn't sure exactly what she was promising, so it wasn't entirely *authentic*. Even though it sounded great, we weren't sure it was *doable*. (The promise to "double" anything is rarely *doable*, so be careful if you hear yourself saying those words.) It was based on *actual sales results* rather than on effort—but we didn't know what those results were, so it wasn't *specific*. It was *defined by a date*, kind of, but it's better to say "July 31" than "the end of July." There is wiggle room in "the end of July." Does it mean "the last week of," "the last business day of," "sometime between June and July," or what?

Fran's promise to double her income in one month was risky. I suggested that she start smaller, and promise more after she had won with small promises. She frowned.

"What if you get the flu, and can't work for three or four days?" I asked her.

"Then I wouldn't make it," she said.

"Can you guarantee you won't get the flu? Or that, even if you got sick and kept going, that you'd be effective? Or that you won't need to take those days off for some other reason?"

Fran began to see what it meant to make the promise. "Oh," she said slowly. "You mean, what do I *really* promise…"

Exactly. When you make "really" promises, your word becomes golden. When your word is golden, you live in an entirely different way. You have a level of confidence that isn't possible when you're leaning back, wondering if you're going to keep the promise. You honor yourself, and how you sell.

The first thing Fran did was to go back and see what she had made in June.

"If I'm honest," she said, "I can guarantee to increase that by 10%."

"Is that realistic? Can you do that without making yourself crazy?" I asked.

"Yes," she said. Her voice was different, and her answers were coming from a less frenetic, more authentic place within her. So now we had *authentic* and *doable*.

"I promise to sell $11,000 by July 31," she said. That gave us actual *sales results*, *specific numbers*, and *defined by a date*.

Make some practice promises. Go over each one to make sure it has all five elements. This is a good exercise to do with a friend. You can usually see the holes in someone else's promise more easily than you can see the holes in your own. Crafting these elegant promises becomes second nature very quickly.

THE SOUL OF SELLING CHANT

Making promises can be daunting. Sometimes we have to ease ourselves into it. If you haven't been making these kinds of commitments, you may experience a certain level of "promise shock." The symptoms of promise shock include near paralysis at the thought of promising *anything* "no matter what," and mental chatter overload.

In the seminar, we use the Soul of Selling Chant to recover from the initial promise shock and muster our courage to make the first promise. I stand on a chair and ask those who still have muscle control to stand as well. With the words written on the easel, we begin softly, rhythmically:

"Complaint to contribution,
Drama to dreams,
Struggle to service,
Reasons to results!"

The beat gets louder. People start to gesture and sway. Sometimes a conga line forms and we march around the room. Whatever it takes to make those promises ...

This is what the chant means:

Complaint to contribution

Promises almost always elicit complaints from mental chatter:

- ▶ Why do I have to do this? Other people don't have to do this.
- ▶ I haven't had a day off in three weeks!
- ▶ I'm moving to the desert and living off the land!

Remember that this kind of complaining is just mental chatter's natural reaction to change, and to getting specific. It's just afraid of risk. Pat it on the head and focus your attention elsewhere.

One of the things that prompted me to develop the Soul of Selling was that I caught myself complaining so often. I wanted to get great results and to contribute. But the more energy I put into complaining, the less I had left for results and contribution. That is how "Complaint to contribution" became part of the chant.

Drama to dreams

There is a catch to the Soul of Selling promises: You can't get dramatic and crazy about them. I know it's not fair, but there it is.

Drama is exciting, but it'll kill you—or at least give you burnout. Drama is a quick fix, a cheap thrill. It's exciting in the short term, but it exacts a terrible price in terms of health, self-esteem, sanity and endurance.

It is the drama we create around keeping our promises that makes them difficult to keep. I spent years being the heroine in the white hat who gave her all, nearly killed herself, and always rode in at the last minute to save the day, or the company, with a great statistic. The last time I did this, I spent two days on the phone with a 103 degree temperature to fill a workshop with six hours to spare. I was a heroine at the organization for which I was selling, but I would never do that today. I would start weeks in advance and never let myself get to two days before a workshop without doing what I had promised to do.

For those of us who have "thrived" on chronic drama, the shift to putting our energy into realizing our dreams can be a challenge. It feels dull. It feels ordinary. We feel just like everybody else, and *that's* certainly not very exciting! We are used to scenarios in which somehow the world is about to end, and we ride in at the last minute to save it with our last ounce of strength. Of course, we have no energy left to pursue or enjoy our dreams—but, hey, it was exciting!

In the years since I've been pursuing dreams instead of drama, I have gotten far more exciting results and have actually seen life as something to be enjoyed, rather than as something to be survived.

Struggle to service

When I was struggling, I couldn't serve people. All my attention was on myself, and I forgot to respect and honor them. I might get the sales result, but I was so exhausted that I didn't have the energy to appreciate people. Struggle was a subset of the chronic drama. "Look what I overcame to get this done!" I would tell people, aloud or just with my attitude. "I rode in at the last minute and saved the day!" A lot of my identity was connected to struggling, and then winning. It was tough to let this go. I had to find other things with which to identify, like enjoying what I did and being truly present with people. People were much better served when I was relaxed, and had the energy and inclination to be gracious with them.

Reasons to results

My first sales mentor always said, "You have your choice in life. You can have the results you want, or you can have the reasons you don't have those results." I hated it! Wasn't she human? Didn't she have any compassion? Just because she could get an 83% statistic selling to a room with 3,000 people in it, didn't she realize we weren't all like that? My fellow mentees and I voiced these objections in a number of angry and pathetic ways.

She simply smiled. She knew it was true, and so did we. She was just waiting for us to get over our snits so we could get out there and use the information to our advantage.

There are always reasons not to keep a promise. Good ones! But without the commitment to results instead of reasons, success is hit-or-miss.

The Soul of Selling Chant may sound silly, but it helps me get inspired and enthusiastic about making promises. We have a choice about whether to complain or contribute, whether to engage our drama or our dreams, whether to deal in struggle or service, and whether we get reasons or results. The doorway to the good stuff—contribution, dreams, service and results—is through promises.

FOUR QUICK "FIXES" FOR "PROMISE PROBLEMS"

If mental chatter is screaming so loudly that you are having trouble making your promise, use one or all of these four quick "fixes":

1. *Stop the music.* When I'm struggling, complaining, being dramatic, or giving reasons why I might not keep my promise—even before

I've actually made it—I know something is out of kilter. The first thing I do is stop. Stopping the downward spiral is as simple as taking a deep breath and saying to yourself, *Wow, I'm starting into a downward cycle. I'm going to stop and write down everything I'm thinking.*

2. *Choose grace under pressure.* Ask yourself if you would rather be a person who demonstrates grace under pressure, or a person known for complaining, drama, struggle, or reasons. If you choose the former, shift your attention, take a deep breath and make your promise.

3. Ask *What am I missing here?* What value do you need to remember about making promises? What's in it for you? What are the benefits to you in making your promise?

4. *"Nike" your promise.* Just do it. Write it down. Sometimes it's just as simple as that. Once you have the promise written down, it may not even seem hard to keep.

These "fixes" all begin with shifting your attention—from complaint to contribution, from drama to dreams, from struggle to service, and from reasons to results. You simply ask yourself which is more important, the complaint or the contribution you can make to your contacts, your family and friends and yourself? The drama, or the dreams of selling big and having all the financial, emotional, spiritual and social rewards that keeping your promise can bring you? The struggle, or the service to your contacts when you see the best in them? The reasons you can't keep your promise, or the rewards and self-esteem you experience when you get the result?

Congratulations! Making your promise is an enormous step. Use these exercises to practice the craft.

EXERCISES

EXERCISE #1: Practice crafting three promises. You are not actually making these promises; you're just practicing how to design promises that are authentic; doable; for sales results, not effort; for specific numbers; and defined by dates. After you've written your promises, check to make sure they have all five elements.

EXERCISE #2: Make one promise. Write it down, and tell a friend about it.

EXERCISE #3: In one column, make a list of everything that could get in the way of you keeping the promise. In another column, make a list of what you will do if that obstacle arises.

EXERCISE #4: Design a reward for yourself for keeping your promise. What will you do, or give yourself?

CHAPTER 9

Step #5:
Conduct the Ten-Touchstone
Honoring Sales Conversation

Everything you've done so far has prepared you for this moment. You've been working behind the scenes, clearing away the old baggage, replacing it with positive personal values, creating your Speaking Bank and making your promise. Now you are ready for action.

The Honoring Sales Conversation is the heart of the Soul of Selling. It ensures that you bring everything you have to the table, and that you treat people with respect and appreciation. It gives you a map of the terrain between Point A and Point B—between "hello" and a clear decision whether or not to buy, made in a supportive, honoring environment that you create.

THE TEN TOUCHSTONES

The Honoring Sales Conversation has ten touchstones. These are checkpoints along the way from Point A to Point B. If you touch each of these markers, you can guarantee that you have given people everything they need, and that you have served them in a way that makes both of you feel good.

We'll go through the touchstones in order, and I suggest that you use them in order at first—particularly if you are new to sales. But once you've mastered them, feel free to use them in whatever order the situation warrants. You can be creative about how you travel the terrain between Point A and Point B, as long as you connect with each of these ten touchstones at some point along the way.

TOUCHSTONE #1: SEE PEOPLE'S VALUE.

This is the most important touchstone, and the basis for everything we do.

What does it mean?

The Soul of Selling is based on the belief that every human being deserves to be respected, honored and appreciated. It assumes that positive qualities such as love, courage, wisdom and good intentions exist in all of us—however obscured they may be at any given moment by fear or stress, and by whatever questionable behavior these discomforts may trigger.

You may or may not know the specific people with whom you'll be talking, but you do know that they will be human beings in whom these qualities exist, regardless of how they feel or how they behave when you speak with them. This touchstone asks you to see those good qualities, and to focus on them no matter what people say or do, and whether or not they buy. It asks you to look beyond the fear or stress and intentionally call forth your appreciation.

Paradoxically, the more you hold this high ground for them, the better their behavior is likely to be.

Where do you get the appreciation?

In Step #2, you made a list of the values you were willing to see in each of your contacts. This is where you bring it. That list tells you what you are willing to appreciate in people, and you can add to it at any time.

Your list may include: loving, intelligent, has dreams in life, wants to contribute, is willing to be vulnerable enough to talk to me about this product or service, or whatever you have decided is worthy of honor, respect and appreciation. Even if people do little or nothing to *demonstrate* these qualities while they are with you, you are willing to see and appreciate them.

The next question is: Where *within yourself* do you get the appreciation, especially at those times when mental chatter gets loud? My friend Frank is an attorney, and a master of seeing the value in people. In Step #2, Frank saw that he valued people's courage and openness in contacting him. Most people who call him are distressed in some way, or they wouldn't be calling a lawyer. Frank admires their initiative and their openness to exploring the possibility of working with him.

"I often expect people to be grumpy, or withdrawn, or hostile, or falling apart," he told me. "I just developed the habit of seeing past that to their courage and openness. When they're in good shape, we start out ahead of the game. But it's my job to deal with them in whatever condition they show up. If I react to them out of my own fears that they won't work with me, or my own distress at *their* distress, we all lose. By holding the line for the goodness I see in them, we all get a better result. Even if they don't feel better, *I* feel better about the interaction!"

I asked Frank where in himself he found the capacity to hold that high ground, and to look beyond his potential clients' apparent hostility or withdrawal. "I just look beyond it," he said. "Like looking beyond my son getting a D in math to the fact that I love him and want to support him. We all get scared, or anxious, or huffy from time to time. I do, anyway. And when I'm scared or anxious, I act weird. When people are like that with me, I just treat them the way I would want to be treated. I want people to look beyond my weird behavior to my good qualities, so I do that with them.

"But there's a selfish part of it, too. At the end of the day, I feel better if I've looked past people's fear to their goodness. I know it's there in them, just like it's there in me. I feel better about myself when I see it. And bottom line, I know I get more of those people as clients. So this is a good, honorable thing to do, I feel better about myself for behaving this way—but it also makes my bottom line better. What's not to like?"

I rest my case.

What you get from Touchstone #1, and how you get it

Touchstone #1 ensures that you feel good about yourself for two reasons:

1. *You behave well.*
2. *You enjoy these conversations.* Can you recall a situation in which you felt honored, respected and appreciated? It was probably very pleasant. You may not have noticed, but it was probably pleasant for the *other* person as well. People who generate these kinds of conversations usually get at least as much benefit as the person with whom they speak.

How do you become the kind of person who generates these conversations? It's easier than you might imagine. You just decide to do it, and use the Honoring Sales Conversation as a guide. My client Pam had very little experience with creating conversations that were honoring and appreciative—but the minute she saw the effect of *not* creating them, she became very skilled almost overnight.

Pam sells a one-day workshop on how to use your PDA most effectively, and last year quit her job to make this workshop her primary source of income. She is a techno-wizard, a great teacher, and wonderful in front of the room, but she was having some difficulty selling the seminar. When we talked, it was clear that she had a great product and the means to deliver it. She was talking to all the right people, but not getting good results from her sales presentations. I pressed her a little about what was happening, and she said, "Hey, take it easy. You're just like those people who don't buy the workshop, always looking for the downside!"

This was a clue. If Pam got as reactive with her contacts as she had with me, they probably wouldn't want her in front of their people—no matter how good her information was, or how well she presented it. I suggested this to her, carefully wrapped in very soft velvet, making sure I saw all the wisdom and talent I'd decided to appreciate in her when I did Step #2.

She just looked at me for a minute. Then she relaxed, and said, "You know, you're right. I wouldn't hire me, either. I wouldn't want me messing with my people."

Pam was a brilliant woman. When she saw that what she was doing was not working, she immediately shifted gear. With minimal coaching, she learned to see people as eager to learn, enthusiastic about sharing what she could give them with their employees, and open to what she had to say—regardless of how distressed or frustrated they might be with their PDAs or technology in general. She chose to look beyond that frustration to their openness, and to the fact that they were willing to talk with her. She became the eye of their storm, and that was very attractive.

"It didn't take long to get on top of this," she said, "because it was actually fun. I had a lot better time dealing with people on that level than I did getting pissed off. Now I can feel compassionate when people say stuff that used to make me crazy. It's like building a muscle. The more I do it, the better I get at it and the easier it gets."

With this piece in place, Pam's business took off.

Devil and Angel

We're all human. When people don't do what we want them to do, sometimes we want to pitch a fit. As sellers, we want people to buy. No matter how much we see the good in them, we would still rather they bought what we are offering. If they don't buy, or even if they hesitate, the mental chatter can get loud. Fortunately, our good instincts are just as strong, and just as loud.

Sometimes I feel as if I have a little devil on one shoulder mouthing all the mental chatter, and a little angel on the other shoulder holding tight to Touchstone #1. As loud as the devil gets, the angel wants just as much to appreciate and connect with other people. These two little cartoon characters are probably sitting on my shoulder all the time, but both of their voices get louder when I sell. Somebody has to step in and referee the situation. That somebody is me. And *you*, the mature person who—just for the duration of the Honoring Sales Conversation—is willing to be the adult, to take a stand for the good and to serve whoever is before you.

The little devil might say, "Jeez, I've see this kind of woman a million times and they never buy. She's gonna take all my time and energy, and then walk away. It happens every time!"

The little angel perks up and says, "Hey, give her a break. What do you know from just looking at her? How about assuming she's just a little shy or scared? How about appreciating her enough to make this situation less intimidating for her? Give her a fighting chance to buy."

"Yeah, but that's not true and you know it," the little devil pipes up defensively.

"Oh, c'mon. What can you appreciate about her? You're just helping yourself. You'll have a better chance for the sale, you'll feel better about yourself, and so will she if you come at this positively."

If you don't let the little angel win, you are in for a frustrating life in sales. I'm not saying the angel has to win all the time, in every aspect of your life. My little angel almost never wins where apple fritters are concerned. But you must let that angel win when you are conducting the Honoring Sales Conversation. That's your covenant with the Soul of Selling. If the angel doesn't win, you're not practicing the Soul of Selling.

When you have this touchstone in place and are seeing people's value, everything that follows is easier and more pleasant. Enjoy what follows, but don't go on automatic. Stay awake. Your angel may be beaming and expanding, but after a few minutes you may see the tips of those little horns starting to climb back over your other shoulder. If that happens, just shift your attention back to the angel. Your job is to make sure the angel is running the show as long as the Honoring Sales Conversation is going on.

TOUCHSTONE #2:
MAKE THIS VALUE THE FOUNDATION OF YOUR CONVERSATION, WHETHER OR NOT THEY BUY.

Touchstone #1 was about calling forth and intentionally appreciating the value in people. Touchstone #2 is about *continuing* to see their value, and to respect and appreciate them, throughout your entire conversation—even if they walk away without buying. It says that you are the adult, the one who guarantees the respect and honor, regardless of what happens. As in Touchstone #1, you are the primary beneficiary. It does more for you than it does for them, because it guarantees your enjoyment.

Buying can be as uncomfortable as selling is. People aren't always at their best when they show up to consider buying. They can get defensive, sullen, or even belligerent. Remember, they probably have at least as much baggage about buying and selling as you did. But the chances of their having done Step #1—Put down your baggage—are slim to none. And Slim just left town. Most likely, the negative chatter about selling (and those who do it!) is still roaming free in their minds.

Your first impulse may be to strike back, but we all know that this usually produces a bad result—and almost inevitably, a result that is not a sale. Paradoxically, *your best antidote to their negative chatter is to honor and appreciate them.* You don't even have to say anything. In fact, engaging them in a discussion of how unaffected you are by their mental chatter would probably be counterproductive. Instead, just *be* the honor and appreciation. Watch the mental chatter scamper around and around on the hamster wheel in their minds, and continue to see the best in them. The worst thing that can happen is that they walk away shaking their heads about what an unusual encounter they had with you.

If you find your appreciation flagging, just get back on the horse. Negative or fearful thoughts may flicker up. Just gently put them aside and return to the respect, honor and appreciation. Let the angel win.

No gushing or squishing!
People are sometimes afraid that this touchstone will make them all gushy, squishy, or placating, and cause them to lose their edge. Exactly the opposite is true.

First of all, getting gushy, squishy, or placating does not honor your contact. We're not talking about flattering people. In fact, that might actually make many of your contacts quite uncomfortable. This touchstone is simply about standing clearly and confidently, even quietly, in the knowledge that your contacts are valuable human beings—and that they remain so, regardless of whether or not they buy.

Diane sells art from her gallery. "Of everything in the Soul of Selling, this was the most valuable to me," she said. "I've always been successful, but I'm enjoying it for the first time. I can relax now because I'm not trying to figure out what they want from me and how to make them feel important. I'm not flattering them. I'm just genuinely appreciating them. When I stopped trying to make them *think* I honored them, and actually *did* honor them, they seemed to relax. And the truth is, I'm selling more."

When people get concerned that Touchstone #2 will "soften" their presentation too much, I think of the line from Woody Allen's movie *Sleeper*. He plays a health food store owner who wakes up in the future and is offered Boston Cream Pie by the scientists who are caring for him. Instead, he demands wheat germ and other healthy foods. They are mystified. They can't believe that he thinks wheat germ is healthier than pies. One scientist shakes his head and says to the other, "Exactly the opposite of what we now know to be true!"

Far from making your presentation too soft, Touchstone #2 will give it depth.

Yeah, but what if...

Most of your conversations will be very pleasant, but here is how Touchstone #2 can help in difficult situations, when your contacts:

▶ *Argue with you about the value of a product.* They might say, "I've used this brand before. It's a piece of junk," or "I don't see what I could get out of your services." As you practice Touchstone #2, you'll see quickly whether they really find no value in what you are offering, or whether this is just their way of asking you for more benefits. If you have any doubt, ask them. You might say, "I understand that you think this brand's other product was a piece of junk. Are you interested in considering this one, or do you just want to let it go?" You might ask the person who wasn't sure if they could benefit from your services, "If you *were* to use us, what would you *like* to get out of it?" If the service really isn't for them, thank them for listening and back off. If they want more benefits, be gracious. Don't get hooked into an adversarial stance. Just give them more benefits. See through their discomfort to what they really want and who they really are at their best.

▶ *Criticize how you're presenting it.* To practice this touchstone, turn the discussion back to the product or service. "I understand that I may not be saying this in a way that works for you, and I'm sorry. I'd hate for the way I'm presenting it to get in the way of your looking seriously at whether or not this car is for you. What can I tell you about it that would be useful to you?"

▶ *Use language you can't abide.* Either ignore it or, if you really can't stand it, get someone else to help them. "Excuse me, folks, I'm going to need to leave now. Let me set you up with Abby. She'll take good care of you." (Check first with Abby to make sure this is okay with her.)

You don't have to put up with outright abuse, but remember that people usually calm down when you keep seeing the best in them. If they don't, you can always end the conversation respectfully and leave. Ending the interaction is preferable to struggling forward, getting angry yourself, or antagonizing them further.

In any case, making the value you see in them the foundation of your conversation ensures that you have done your best and acted with honor. The most likely outcome is that you experience a wonderful connection.

TOUCHSTONE #3: CONNECT WITH THE PERSON.

Touchstones #1 and #2 are internal. You do them unilaterally. The other person doesn't have to be involved. In Touchstone #3, you create the relationship with your contact. You reach out and establish a connection. This connection happens at an energetic level, and you know when it's there. You relax and smile, at least internally, and so does the other person. You can both feel it.

What makes the connection?

There are many ways to establish this connection. It might be with a handshake, a smile, a nod, a brief greeting, or a general comment about the day, the store, or the friend who introduced you. It can be all of these, or none of them. You can have the handshake, the nod, even the same grandmother—and still not have a connection. These gestures may reflect the connection, but they do not cause it.

The connection comes from within you. It usually occurs naturally as you see value in another person. When people reach out to you with positive regard, don't you usually respond? You may not say or do anything, but the connection is there. Why wouldn't you want to connect with someone who is seeing you that way? When you reach out energetically to the other person, seeing the best in them and extending yourself in some physical way, the connection almost always occurs.

You know when you have it, and when you don't.

Wait for the "ping."

When you connect with another person, you can usually feel a "ping." Spiritual healers sometimes call this moment "registration." The connection "registers" with both of you, whether or not the other person is consciously aware of it. It's as if you are figuratively (and sometimes, literally) standing beside the other person with your arm around their shoulder, looking together at what you're offering. You are colleagues, on the same team, with a common goal to determine whether or not your product or service is right for them.

I don't want to make this more complicated than it is, but one of the most frequent mistakes people make is launching into a presentation before the connection has actually occurred. They get so excited about the product or service, or so anxious to make the sale, that they surge ahead of themselves. They're off down the toboggan slope, but they don't have the other person on the sled with them.

TOUCHSTONE #4: SHARE YOUR VISION.

People need to know what you are offering, and they expect that it will be be presented in the best way possible. You owe it to yourself, to them, and to your product or service to give them that. This is where you use your Speaking Bank.

Start the conversation with your opening ten-second sound bite. Your instincts will tell you what to say next. Notice what impact your words are having on the other person. If people appear to "go away" mentally, ask them a question—even if it's only, "Is this making sense? Am I covering the information you need to know?" Keep them with you. Move through your Speaking Bank intuitively until you've given them everything they need in order to buy. Remember to keep honoring them and holding their interest.

Most of the time, you'll be engaged in two-sided conversations. There may be times, however, when you are asked to give a short presentation before answering questions. Ruth was the newly named capital campaign chair at her church. She had no sales experience, and was faced with a series of "at home" meetings. The idea was that at each of these meetings, she would present the vision of the new church to between three and six people, answer their questions, and then ask them for a donation.

This was a challenge for her, but she said, "I just flung myself into the pool and decided I had to swim. The Speaking Bank was my lifesaver. I had all these good things to say, and I memorized them. So then I just looked at those folks and reached for whatever sound bite felt right. After a while, I could just tell what they needed to hear to get inspired. You know, it was much easier than I thought it'd be. Each group was different, but it always came out clearer than I thought it would." Ruth became a force of nature in that capital campaign.

This touchstone is about letting it rip. Keep an eye on the other person and make course corrections if necessary—but mostly, have fun talking about what you offer. You are taking a stand for your product or service, for the best in the people with whom you speak and for the best in yourself. That feels great.

TOUCHSTONE #5: FIND OUT THE VALUE TO THEM.

This is where you find out what your contacts want. If they bought your product or service, what would they want it to do for them? You need this information for four reasons:

- ▶ *You need to see whether there is a match between what they want and what you have*, and to direct them to the best application of your product or service. You may have several models of a product, or several different forms of service. Knowing what they want helps you point them to the most useful choice—the right insurance terms, copier model, coaching format, etc. If there is no match between what they want and what you have, you both are better off knowing it.
- ▶ *They need to hear themselves say it.* People usually know they want *something*, but they may not know exactly *what it is* until somebody asks them and they have to say it out loud. It's a little like staring into the refrigerator, knowing you want something in there,

but not being able to focus on any one thing. When they hear themselves say what they want, everything gets clearer for them and they move closer to the sale. If they are ready to buy, it gives them the green light to go ahead. After they have bought, they are happier if they know precisely what need has been satisfied. That translates into minimal post-sale difficulties like returns and complaints, and is your best source for referrals and repeat business. You are the one who made it all clear for them, by asking the right questions.

▶ *If they start wavering, you need to know where to return.* When people bring up objections, you will hear them. But at some point, you will turn the conversation back to the value that your product or service holds for them.

▶ *They need some value to weigh against what it costs them.* They need to know what they want, so they can put it on the other side of the imaginary scale from what it will cost them. Oddly, it rarely occurs to people to do this. You usually have to suggest it.

The Power of the Hypothetical

Sometimes I think people lapse into a light trance when they are considering buying. They seem to enter a netherworld where it may not even occur to them to think about what they want from your product or service. You can snap them out of that trance, and keep both of you on track, by asking questions like these:

▶ If you were to do this workshop, what might you want to get out of it?

▶ What would you like a computer to do for you?

▶ What are the advantages to you of the sedan over the coupe?

▶ Your eyes light up when you talk about the five-day program. What do you see as the value there?

These are crucial questions, but you need to ask them gently. Don't pound on people or appear to be confronting them. Use qualifiers like "might," "would," and "if," as in these examples. That makes the question hypothetical, and hypothetical questions are safer. You are looking together at a range of possibilities, all of which are at some distance, rather than pressing them into what they might perceive as a semi-commitment.

Here is how it works. Consider these two questions:

> ▶ If you were to do this, what might you want from it?
> ▶ What need of yours will this satisfy?

You are asking for the same information in these two questions, but you are much more likely to get it from the first one. The first question is safer, and therefore easier for them to answer.

"At first I found myself not wanting to ask the 'value question,'" George told me. "I guess I was afraid they really didn't see any value. So I didn't want to press that button. But now I love it. It gets them into their own enthusiasm, and that builds my enthusiasm. It gets the conversation on a very positive footing. If they really don't see any value, we both know it and can move on!"

If they do see a value, you can move on to Touchstone #6.

TOUCHSTONE #6: INVITE THEM TO PARTICIPATE.

This is where you pop the question.

> ▶ Would you like to register for the Bronze Plan?
> ▶ Shall we get you signed up for the January workshop?
> ▶ Would you like to make an appointment?
> ▶ Shall we ring this up for you?

For many people, this is the best part of the conversation. They love it, because it opens the door for people to say "Yes." It brings completion, and is usually a "win" for everybody.

For other people, "the ask" is agony. They forget about the ecstasy on the other side of the question—the "Yes!"—and focus instead on their discomfort. Most people who don't like "the ask" give one of two reasons:

1. They're afraid of being too pushy.
2. They open the door to "No."

Let's look at the first reason first:

Releasing Fear of Pushiness

Fear of pushiness is a little carry-on baggage that slipped through Step #1. You may have been told as a child not to be pushy. It's not polite. You may have been pushed by other people, and not liked it.

Fear of Pushiness can keep you stuck. Whatever negative associations you have with pushiness or "the ask," it's good to identify what they are and put down that carry-on. In a way, this becomes a mini-Step #1. Here are some tools for moving beyond it:

1. *Recognize that you have to ask the question at some point.* This is where the sale is made. You can't hear "Yes" until you ask the question. There's no point in doing anything else if you aren't going to ask people if they want what you are offering. Given that you need to ask the question, how can you make this a positive experience for yourself and for your contact?

2. *Recognize that if you aren't pushing, people won't feel pushed.* If you're tense, nervous, and dreading the ordeal, people will sense that—and they may seize up as well. Quite apart from whether or not they want what you are offering, their emotional reaction is likely to mirror yours to some degree. The more comfortable you are with "the ask," the more comfortable they will feel about giving you their answer—whatever that answer is.

3. *Choose how you want this question to come across,* and practice delivering it that way.

The first thing I ever sold on a large scale was a workshop. I used to agonize when it came time for "the ask." This is the kind of thing that used to run through my mind: "Oh my God, I'm asking them for money they don't have and don't really want to give. They'll either say 'No' and make fun of me, or 'Yes' and hate me. Either way, they'll think I'm a pushy shyster and my relationship with them will be reduced to me breaking their arms and legs to get them to do something they really don't want to do and being a bad person. Then I'll go to hell…" I'll be merciful and stop there, but rest assured that this was only the beginning.

Then a strange thing began to happen. As I postponed "the ask" in conversations, people got impatient. Sometimes they even interrupted me and said, "Look, I've heard enough. What do I have to do to sign up?" I realized that in trying to avoid or delay that moment, I was disturbing the flow of the conversation. They were ready and I wasn't paying attention. Instead, I was paying attention to my own discomfort. That was making everything harder for both of us.

When I thought about what had happened, I realized that "the ask" was actually much more uncomfortable for me than it was for them. *People expect to be asked to buy.* They anticipate it. Our foreboding is much greater than theirs. It is a normal part of sales conversations.

I also realized that avoiding "the ask" was like calling someone up and talking about the dinner party you were throwing—and then not inviting them! *You* might know you wanted them to come, and they might even assume it at some level, but the conversation has an uncomfortable quality until you actually say the words, "Would you like to come on Friday night?"

Even when you don't get a "Yes," their answer tells you where you are in the selling process. If they need more information, or if they need to voice more objections, "the ask" will bring that forward. Inviting them to participate is the ultimate "Yeah, but"—solicitor—and you need to get those "Yeah, buts" up into the light of day. More about that in the next touchstone.

Releasing Fear of "No"

Another reason some people dread "the ask" is that they don't want to hear "No." I've heard all kinds of antidotes to The Fear of "No," and they've come from everyone from clinical psychologists to discount superstore salespeople. These answers can get very complex and very deep, and the results are hit-and-miss.

The one antidote I've seen work every time is this: *Don't take it personally*. It sounds simple, and it is. Simple, but not always easy.

In the seminar, I illustrate not taking it personally by asking someone to come up and stand with me. I put my arm around their shoulder, as we do figuratively when we talk with contacts. Then I pick up a box of tissues from the table and hold it out at arm's length. "Now this is one great box of tissues," I say. "It has beautiful colors, and the tissues are soft on your face. My favorite thing about this box is that it's square and not oblong. If you were to buy this box of tissues, what would you want to get out of it?"

After this quick tap on the first five touchstones, I ask the person to refuse to buy the box of tissues, and even to be vehement about how it would not work for him. He acts out a strong refusal, and I practice not taking it personally. He has rejected the tissues, and yet he and I are still standing there together, talking about something that is outside both of us. He's not rejecting *me*. I'd rather he had bought the tissues, but his "No" doesn't take anything away from me, or from our relationship. There are millions more people with whom I can speak about the tissues, and I'll have a good time doing it.

Think of what you are selling as the box of tissues. They are not saying "No" to *you*. They are saying "No" to *it*. You are looking *with* them at the tissue box. You are supporting them in making a choice about it.

The dynamic of choice goes on between them and the box, not between them and you. Most of the time, they are not even "rejecting" your product or service. It's just not right for them at that point, or there is something else that suits their needs better. Or they have no good reason; they just don't want it. No problem. It has nothing to do with you.

Many times, I've known that people thought I was terrific—but they simply didn't want or need what I was offering. And I've sold to people I know did not like me personally, but who did like what I was offering. You just can't take it personally, either way.

When you learn not to take "No" personally, you lose your fear of it.

TOUCHSTONE #7:
HEAR THEIR OBJECTIONS
WITHOUT GETTING HOOKED.

Objections are all the reasons people give for not being able or willing to buy. When you ask people if they want to buy, the first things out of their mouths are usually their objections. This is a good thing! You want to surface those objections. Until people have a chance to voice them, the objections lay hovering beneath the surface—keeping them stuck where they are and preventing them from buying. Or they may buy, but they'll return it later.

What do objections look like?

Objections often take the form of not having enough money or enough time...or of wanting what you are offering, but "later." They sound like this:

▶ That's a great TV, but I don't have the money right now.
▶ Your package for our company looks good, but we just can't afford it.
▶ Consulting sounds wonderful, but I'm too busy right now to take on anything else.
▶ We'd like you to do the work on our carpets, but we're in the middle of reorganizing and don't have time for anything else. Let me get back to you when the dust settles.
▶ We're expecting a great third quarter. I'll call you when the funds are available.
▶ I'd like to do a makeover, but I want to lose ten pounds first.

Whether these objections are true or not doesn't matter. At this point, all that matters is that you have surfaced them. Any objections left in the back of their minds will fester and turn into negative mental chatter.

Steam coming out of your ears

Frustration and irritation can be natural first responses to hearing objections. You may think people are flat out lying to you. You may think they're wimps for not moving forward. You may just be angry because you have a promise to keep, and they're not helping. In any case, you feel thwarted!

Fortunately, we don't act on these initial responses in the Soul of Selling. We take a deep breath, and revisit Touchstones #1 and #2. We get back in touch with what we are willing to honor and appreciate in people.

When I first started selling, I wasn't very good at dealing with objections. I wanted to say, "You liar! I know you really have the money and the time. You're just lazy and don't want to be uncomfortable. Don't try to pull one over on me!" For the most part, I was wise enough to bite my tongue. But I churned inside, and lived in an almost constant state of resentment.

In Alcoholics Anonymous, they say, "Resentment is like taking poison and expecting the other person to die." Eventually, I realized that my reactions were hurting me more than they were hurting anybody else. If I continued down that path, several things might happen. I might actually start saying these things out loud, and lose every sale. I might continue to stuff back the reactions, and be miserable. Or I might get passive aggressive, and smile while I sent little mental daggers at these poor people. One way or the other, I was going to have a terrible time selling. And people who have a terrible time selling generally don't do well at it.

The solution was to change my response. The first thing I had to do was stop taking the objections personally, just as I had learned to stop taking "No" personally. "I don't have the time," may mean many things, but it has nothing to do with you.

Why they do it

People raise objections for many reasons:

> ▶ *They have genuine concerns,* and need to voice them—if only to themselves. Their objections are sometimes just worries, not insurmountable obstacles that will keep them from buying. "I have no money right now" may really mean, "I'm worried about money.

I don't really know how much I have, but I should probably spend less than I do."

▸ *The objections are coded messages for others.* Before he buys, a man may need for his wife to hear the objection, "We don't really need a sit-down lawn mower." (Translation: I'm not really a wimp; I'm willing to tough it out and keep pushing that hand mower until I drop dead.) The answer he wants is, "Oh, George, go ahead and buy it. We're not getting any younger, and you deserve it after all your hard work!"

▸ *They need to hear themselves say it.* Even when people have every intention of buying, they sometimes need to hear themselves say, "I don't have the time" or "I don't have the money." They know they are going to "change their minds," but they want it stated for the record (yours and their own) that they are not spending the time or money frivolously, without at least giving it some serious thought.

▸ *They are trying to be polite.* They don't want what you are offering, but think it would be rude to come out and tell you that. They don't want to hurt your feelings, and they don't want to be embarrassed. It is their polite way of saying "No." They believe that "I'd love to do it, but I just can't" is more compassionate, and less likely to hurt your feelings, than "I don't want it." In this case, their primary concern is to save your feelings—and that is kind, if somewhat confusing.

▸ *They really don't have the time or money.* Sometimes people honestly cannot afford what you are offering, or don't have the time to do it. Buying simply isn't appropriate for these people. Let them go with respect and appreciation.

You may never know which of these conditions is true for your contacts, and it really doesn't matter. You proceed in the same way regardless of what they say, or whether or not it is actually true. You see the best in them, hear the objection down to your toes, don't buy into it, don't take it personally, and begin to explore with them whether or not the objection is going to prevent them from buying.

"Clearing" objections

"Clearing" an objection means that people get beyond it and buy. They go from having no money at all to, "Well, I suppose I could ask Uncle Albert for the money," or "I do have that 'rainy day' account," or "I guess I could switch some things around."

How do you support people in going beyond their objections, if that's the appropriate thing for them to do? There are four steps:

1. *Don't try to argue them out of their objections.* This only gives them something to resist, and makes the objection "stick." Imagine if somebody said to you, "Oh, come on. I know you really have the money." I'd want to dig in my heels, and that's what most people do.

2. *Make them feel heard.* The way you do this is by really hearing them. Sometimes all people need is for someone to hear that they have a concern about buying. The minute that happens, they are over it and no longer cling to the objection. If they keep repeating themselves, it is a clue that they don't feel heard.

3. *Don't get hooked.* Understand that their objection is of concern to them, but don't jump to the conclusion that it is true, or that it will prevent them from buying. Just be a listening post, without making any decisions. Respect their concerns—but don't go down the garden path with them without making further inquiries.

4. *Give them a choice.* You might say something like, "I understand that money is at a premium right now, and you have to choose carefully where you invest it. So let's look again at whether or not this is worth it to you. You told me that you want (whatever it is) from this insurance policy. On the other hand, it costs $375. Let's put these two things on an imaginary scale and see what you really want to do." The person feels heard and honored. You respect that there is a decision to be made here, and you've clarified what the choice is.

If they really want what you're offering and it is a good choice for them, the objection will clear. If particular objections tend to "stick" with your contacts, it is sometimes useful to look in the mirror.

The Mirror

There is no scientific proof for this, but my empirical evidence suggests that when we have baggage about time, money, or anything else—that baggage tends to be reflected in our contacts' objections. Sellers with time baggage tend to hear a lot of time objections. Sellers with money baggage tend to hear a lot of money objections.

We all have different "stop points," or particular objections that tend to "stick" around us. My friend Rosemary is a master seller, but her "stop point" is money. When her contacts have objections about money, they don't clear as easily as objections about time do. With me, it's the opposite. Objections about money usually clear quickly and easily, but objections about time have a tendency to stick. I know that I have a lot more baggage about time than I do with money.

I've heard all kinds of explanations for this mirroring phenomenon. Metaphysical types say, "What you resist, persists. You draw to you from the universe conditions that mirror what you yourself need to handle." Psychological types say, "Unconsciously you don't work as hard to clear objections if you secretly agree with them. That would invalidate your own refusals." One very successful truck salesman told me, "Dumb luck, I guess."

I have no clue why this happens, but I have observed over thirty years of selling that it does—and that it is an opportunity. Whenever objections about time rear their head around me, I adopt the point of view that I need to ease up on my own nervousness about not having enough time. I take a deep breath, and let go. I might call someone and schedule a social coffee to relax. The minute I see what is happening and take action to clear my own time worries, the objection stops "sticking."

Course Corrections

This is what I call a course correction. You see that what you are doing isn't working, and you do something else. You look for what might work instead, and you give it a try. If that doesn't work, you make another course correction. You try something else.

We've all heard that when a plane flies from San Francisco to Hawaii, it's only directly on course about 3% of the time. Life is a series of course corrections, and in selling we have abundant opportunities to practice.

When you've heard their objections without buying them, you can move on to Touchstone #8.

TOUCHSTONE #8: TAKE THEM BACK TO THE VALUE.

After you have heard their objections, take people back to basics, to the value that they see in your product or service. Ask them again what they want it to do for them, or remind them of what they said earlier. Don't be afraid to repeat this part of the journey. It's the most important segment. This is always safe territory, a place for both you and your contact to rest, relax and enjoy.

It might look like this: You've established your connection and asked what they would like to get out of using you as their architect. They've told you they love your style, and that you seem to have been inside their heads and known just what they wanted.

"We'd love to work with you," Mrs. Jones says, "but you are a bit more expensive than Smith and Smith. I'm just not sure we can afford you."

You smile. You're seeing the best in them. (Because they are a couple, you give them equal attention, credence and weight. Regardless of who makes the decision, this is good business. If they make decisions jointly, it is essential.) You nod in understanding. You hear them.

"I know we're a little more of an investment," you say, "and that you want to do this as economically as possible. But I agree that we're on the same wavelength. Only you know what that's worth to you. I invite you to consider that, and weigh it against the slightly higher fee. Tell me again exactly what you would want if you did wind up using our firm."

The Joneses are now back in the visioning stage, but you can't take them there unless you've first made it clear to them that you have heard their objection about money. In the end, what people really have to do is put the value they want on one side of the scale, and the cost on the other.

The Scale

We've talked about the scale. It's a very simple, and very handy, metaphor to use with people who aren't clear immediately whether or not they want to buy. Value on one side, cost on the other. It makes their decision easier, and it is a godsend for any seller who has experienced angst as they near the close of the sale. You're not pitching. You're not cajoling or manipulating. You're suggesting a simple exercise that brings people to an honest and clear decision. What they want on one side, what it costs on the other. It's that easy, and people will love you for it.

TOUCHSTONE #9: CLOSE THE SALE.

Closing the sale means asking clearly whether or not they want to buy, and getting a clear "Yes" or "No."

What you can, and can't, control

You can control some elements of the "close." You can control how much honor and respect you put into the environment in which they make their choice. You can fill that environment with appreciation without saying a word. They will know exactly how you are seeing them, whether or not they can actually articulate it. You can also control how willing you are to hear either "Yes" or "No" without withdrawing your appreciation. That's about all you can control. Hold to the high road with these elements of the close.

You cannot control whether or not they buy. It's their choice. You can influence that choice with the connection, presentation, and the relationship you develop with them. All those things support a "Yes," but they don't guarantee it. In the end, your contacts get to choose. The thing you have to remember is that if they don't buy, someone else will.

Regardless of what they choose, your goal is for them to walk away feeling good about themselves, and good about you. When you least expect it, often years later, people come strolling back because they remembered how nice you were when it wasn't time for them to buy—and now it's time. At the end of the day, you want to feel 100% good about each of your interactions. This stance actually fuels the "Yes" side of their equation, but your primary concern is the relationship.

Closing with ease, grace and dignity

If you are truly in service to the other person, almost anything you say will come out with ease, grace and dignity. You've heard the old phrase, "Who you are is speaking so loudly I can't hear what you're saying." The words you use to close are not as important as the place from which you speak them.

You can ask the same kinds of questions to close the sale as you asked in Touchstone #6. (If there are no objections, Touchstone #6 actually *becomes* the close.)

▶ Shall we get the paperwork done?
▶ Would you like to take it home?
▶ Are you ready to sign up?

Again, don't worry about repeating yourself. People don't notice. All their attention is on themselves, as it should be.

The benefits of closing

If you find yourself getting queasy about closing, and notice that the attention is slipping back to you and how you are doing, remember to shift your focus back to them. Relax into the benefits of closing:

1. *You are no longer in no man's land.* You know whether or not this is a sale. You know where you are with keeping your promise. If they are not going to buy, you can let them go and proceed to the next person. If they do buy, you can celebrate together.

2. *They are no longer in no man's land.* I've had many people thank me for pressing them a little to come to a decision, rather than just "hanging out with it" for a while. It was a relief for *them* to know "Yes" or "No." One woman said, "I didn't want to give you an answer, but if you hadn't kept at me a little and I hadn't finally said 'No,' I would have walked around that whole week knowing I wasn't going to buy but not wanting to tell you. That would have cost me a lot of energy. You did me a real service." If your contacts aren't going to buy, it serves them to tell you so. Then they are no longer hanging out in uncertainty, and *neither are you.* Whether the answer is "Yes" or "No," you both have clarity and resolution.

When to postpone the close

If people absolutely cannot come to a "Yes" or "No," then let them go away for now. But before you let them go, make sure you do two things:

1. *Schedule a specific time to talk and revisit their choice.* The reason you do this is so they won't walk away bleeding energy from a conversation that never came to a conclusion, and neither will you. Make sure you get a specific day and time, and determine who will call whom. Then make sure you both write it in your books, and exchange numbers. They may say, "Let's talk next week." This is too vague. You'll waste time and energy playing phone tag. You can say, "What day works for you?" Then ask them what time works for them. Get to, "Tuesday morning at 10:30. How about if I call you?" If you start with anything less specific than this, the phone tag may take on Olympic proportions, until one or both of you give up.

2. *Give them homework.* Otherwise, you'll start where you left off— nowhere. Ask them to make a list of everything they want from what you're offering, and exactly what it will cost them. Then have them put it on the scale. Your first question after connecting is, "What did you see when you put this on the scale?"

If I don't get a "Yes" at the second meeting, I consider it a "No." I hold the door open, but I don't hold my breath.

The whole point of closing is to resolve your conversation. It comes full circle, and everybody knows where they are. There should be a real sense of peace and completion for both you and your contact after the close.

After the "Yes"—or the "No"

There is sometimes another awkward moment after people have said, "Yes" when you have to get their payment or complete the paperwork. Some sellers get so unnerved by having made the sale that they are overly elated or overly casual about this important part of the deal. Stay calm. Stay connected. Keep honoring them. Yes, you made the sale. You can get it down in your stats later. Yes, you are genuinely excited for them, but they are depending on you to be the steady one who guides them through the rest of the mechanics with calm certainty. Right now, just look them in the eye and let them know that you are genuinely grateful to them for letting you serve them in this way. Then keep serving them by continuing the relationship that was in place when they bought.

If they've said "No," never let your connection with them waver. Keep appreciating them. Respect their decision. Honor the time you spent together. Let them go, and wish them all the best. I've had literally hundreds of people come back to me years later to buy because of how they were treated when they *didn't* buy.

TOUCHSTONE #10:
VALIDATE THEIR CHOICE,
EVEN IF IT'S NOT TO PARTICIPATE WITH YOU.

People who use the Soul of Selling take good care of their contacts. Validating their choice of "Yes" or "No" is part of that care.

Validating their choice simply means that they know you are okay with whatever they have chosen, and honor their decision—whatever it is. You don't have to fall all over yourself if they say "No," and gush, "Oh, you're absolutely right. I could see immediately it wasn't for you!" Just continue to honor them, and thank them for taking the time to talk with you and to consider your product or service. Send them on their way feeling good about themselves. Treat them as you would if you knew you would run into them in a restaurant that night. If there is any queasiness or uneasiness in the space, fix it before they go. Make some gesture of connection: a handshake, a smile, a kind or grateful word.

Being less than honoring with them if they say "No" will not change their answer to "Yes." It can only have a bad, or a neutral, outcome. Being respectful and appreciative when they say "No" can only have a *good* or neutral outcome. Take your pick.

If they say "Yes," it's just as important to validate their decision. Cut "buyer's remorse" off at the pass. Tell them:

▶ I'm so glad you decided to sign up. From what you say, this is a great policy for you.

▶ That coat looks just great on you. I didn't want to gush at you, but I was hoping you'd see what I was seeing.

▶ Congratulations on letting yourself have this. I can tell it's going to bring you a lot of joy.

It doesn't take much to tell them they did a great job of choosing, and it can mean a lot. Think about how you feel when you buy. Doesn't it send you off feeling great if the person who sold to you validates your choice. "That suit is just terrific on you!" When I sold seminars, people often told me, "I remember what you said right after I signed up, about feeling like it was the right time and the right place for me. That kept me going, even when I thought I'd made a mistake and was thinking about withdrawing."

When people say "Yes," be sure you give them anything they might need between the sale and actually attending, taking possession of, or being a part of whatever you're offering. Make sure they walk away with something physical, if only a receipt. If it's appropriate, give them something more: a pamphlet, a guarantee, some paperwork. Also make sure they have your card and know that they can call you if there is any problem.

I once bought a computer from a woman who kept in touch with me and walked me through some customer service problems I had in the first few months. She didn't have to do it, but she ran interference for me with these accounting and support difficulties. I always returned to her for my computer needs. Even after she left the company, I continued to buy that brand of computer.

Remember that people sometimes get nervous after they buy. (Mental chatter is being forced to endure another change!) Help them out with as much validation as you can.

FUN IS THE BOTTOM LINE

The bottom line with the Honoring Sales Conversation is to have fun with it. Relax and enjoy people. There's nobody to impress. Just be yourself. And when in doubt, tell the truth.

Remember that Step #5 is *Conduct* the Honoring Sales Conversation. You are in charge, and you will know instinctively what to say next. Use the touchstones to usher your contacts through an empowering, honoring talk that leads to a good decision about your product or service—and a relationship they will never forget.

Take a moment to do these exercises, then be prepared for the final and most powerful step in the next chapter.

EXERCISES

EXERCISE #1: What do you imagine would be your most uncomfortable moments in the Honoring Sales Conversation? Make a list of them. They might include introducing yourself, delivering points from your Speaking Bank, keeping up the connection in the face of discomfort, the closing, or remaining warm and honoring when people say "No."

EXERCISE #2: What can you do to ease yourself through each of these moments? For each item on your list from Exercise #1, write the antidote. One universal antidote is to put your attention back on the other person. What are others?

What's important to you?

Time for a hobby?   Time with family and friends?

Financial Security?

Are these priorities being met?

If not, let me invite you to look at a way I am buying back my time and creating financial security for my future.

It's true. You use this product every single day. You most likely are overpaying for it. Find out how you can either save money or make money. You decide.

I will share with you a way to improve your financial future while still feeling secure trading time for money in corporate America today.

www.teamltd.energygoldrush.com

Karen Carlson 630.542.7573

CHAPTER 10

Step #6: Keep Going until You Get the Result

Here is where you win. You do what you said you would do, and come home with the prize.

Step #6 means just what it says. You keep having the Honoring Sales Conversation with as many people as it takes to get the result you promised in Step #4. That is a delicious and empowering conversation. Some people spend their whole lives searching for interactions like that, and you get to do it over and over again.

THE HERO'S JOURNEY WITHIN THE HERO'S JOURNEY

Joseph Campbell, the author and mythologist, said that life is richer when we see it as a hero's journey, a series of lessons about waking up and realizing our true nature. If this is so, then selling is *the hero's journey within the hero's journey*.

Life is full of lessons, and selling is even more so. Every day, we have promises to keep—not just promises about sales results, but guarantees that people will be honored, respected and appreciated in our presence. We learn to manage our mental chatter, stay present to the best in people, overcome obstacles and let our inspiration shine through in our conversations with them. That is a hero's journey.

At the same time that we are dealing with our own mental chatter, making course corrections, and keeping ourselves on track, we are also being present to our contacts' mental chatter without buying into it, and putting our own chatter aside in order to provide a safe and supportive environment in which they can make good choices. That is a double journey, a hero's journey within the hero's journey. The Soul of Selling helps you walk this path mindfully, and with the proper equipment, maps, guidelines and support.

Your heroism emerges most clearly in Step #6. This step asks you for your power, your commitment, your ability to be a stand for what you offer, and your willingness to do whatever it takes to succeed in bringing that vision into reality.

This chapter shows you how to take a deep breath and make it all work for you—with joy, and in the spirit of service to your contacts and yourself.

THE DONUT MAN

It was Sunday morning, the last day of the seminar. Everyone was in their seat, ready to start, when the door swung open. A man stood in the doorway wearing a white peaked Krispy Kreme hat and carrying a huge tray of fancy donuts. He held the tray aloft, smiled broadly and said with a flourish, "Good morning, Carol, I'm here to pass some hors d'oeuvres if that's okay."

"As long as you start with me," I said. I selected a donut so hot and creamy it began to melt in my hand. As I savored every gram of deep-fat-fried white flour, every granule of melting sugar, I watched him go around the circle. He looked each person in the eye and smiled. Then he offered them the tray as if it held the greatest treasure on earth. Some people grabbed at the donuts. He smiled and said, "Take another if you like. We have plenty." He handed them a napkin and smiled again. "Enjoy!" he said, and moved to the next person.

The whole group was entranced. They watched him move around the circle, obviously delighted by what he was doing. He filled the room with an energy that made them feel relaxed, cared for, appreciated and celebrated. His enthusiasm and joy were infectious.

Not everybody took the donut he offered. Some people were on a diet, or had just eaten, or were diabetic, or just didn't want one—but they had just as good a time as those who snapped up two donuts. When people said they were on a diet, he beamed, "Good for you. All the best with it!" and moved on. People sat watching, a few of their faces smeared with chocolate or glazed frosting, grinning and transfixed.

The man was Darrel Schmucker, who had taken the seminar a few months earlier. He had called me a few weeks after the seminar to say how well the "hors d'oeuvres tray approach" was working for him. Now here he was, demonstrating exactly what he meant. When he was finished going around the circle, he asked if he could say a few words. I was delighted. I hadn't known he was coming, but I couldn't have said anything that would have given people a better understanding of Step #6 than Darrel just had.

"I knew you'd be talking about Step #6 this morning," he said, "and it's been so great for me that I wanted to give back. I used to give up a lot, and I hated the idea of 'keep going.' But thinking of it as passing the hors d'oeuvres tray worked for me, and now Step #6 is my trump card. I know I'll always win because I have it in my pocket. It's evolved into the Krispy Kreme tray for me—but I wanted to show you how much fun it could be, even for someone who didn't do it naturally. So thanks, and have a great time today. I have one more thing for you before I leave."

With that, he went around the circle and gave everybody a white peaked Krispy Kreme hat like the one he was wearing.

"So you'll remember," he said and waved as he walked out the door. People burst into applause and gave him a standing ovation.

That morning, Darrel was the embodiment of Step #6. He gave everyone in that seminar the gift of seeing it in action. He showed them the perfect attitude in which to do this step. His generosity was the ultimate in Step #6-ness.

THE PLEASURE OF PERSEVERENCE

The key with Step #6 is to keep it light, and keep it fun. People tend to furrow their brows when they first hear, "Keep going until you get the result." They dig in mentally and prepare to be grim, glum and driven. They assume that to keep going is only a small step down from climbing Mt. Everest in winter, or having a root canal.

Step #6 need not be grim. In fact, it should be joyous. Ask Darrel. You are just making one offering, and then another and another. The more you allow yourself the joy of the offering, the fewer times you may have to make it. If you approach it as fun, inspiring and a contribution, Step #6 will be your favorite. It is, after all, the one that guarantees your success. This is the moment when you break the tape at the end of the race!

Here is the secret to Step #6: You can't count on anyone else to inspire you, jack you up, or get you going. People can help you, and Chapter 12 is all about letting yourself be supported, but you have to be the source of that energy. This chapter contains many tips and "fixes" for getting inspired and for reigniting your passion at will.

That's the good news. You are in control. You are in charge of what you think, and where you direct your energy and attention. Go to the positive, and your path will be quicker and easier. If you are willing to be the one who generates the inspiration, enthusiasm, joy and success of this step, I guarantee that you will get the result.

THE BIGGEST POTHOLE
(AND HOW TO STEP AROUND IT)

Step #6 is the Star Trek step. It asks you to go beyond where you may have gone before, and to venture outside of your comfort zone. You may find some new potholes out there in the unknown zone, and the biggest potholes are likely to be excuses. Most of us have used excuses more than we realize.

Jennifer sold memberships at a national health club. When people walked in with questions, they were ushered to Jennifer's office. She was supposed to sit them down and sell them a membership. She had been moderately successful, but her results were erratic. She never knew from one week to the next whether her numbers would be great, terrible, or somewhere in between. Jennifer's boss had talked to her about this, and sent her to the seminar to get some consistency.

"Some weeks are just terrific," she told me. "People walk in ready to sign up, and we sign them up. Other weeks, nobody comes in, and those who do come in don't want to join. I can't control what happens. It just depends on where people are, and if they even come in! I can't do anything if they're, like, not there to talk to!"

Jennifer is not alone. This is most people's attitude when they start selling, and occasionally even after they've been selling for quite some time. When things aren't going well, they look for excuses.

But wait! Aren't there sometimes valid reasons that things aren't going well? Absolutely. But remember that you have a choice. You can have the results you want, or you can have the reasons you don't have them.

Who's in charge here?

It's true that some circumstances favor selling, and other circumstances seem to work against selling. But if you let circumstances determine whether or not you keep going, you are dead in the water. You won't have the experience of knowing, deep within yourself, that you will get the result—no matter what. You will always have an excuse if things don't go well at first. Once you start accepting excuses, the odds of actually getting your result start to plummet.

I'm not saying you should keep going in the face of a broken leg or the death of a family member. Obviously, you'll use common sense. I'm talking about these kinds of excuses:

▶ It's just not the right time of year for people to buy this.
▶ I just couldn't work up the enthusiasm to keep going.
▶ The way this company is run, it's a wonder I can sell *anything*.
▶ Our pricing is off, so it's very hard to sell.
▶ The marketing this company does is all wrong.
▶ I can't help it that people aren't walking in the door. I mean, I can't talk to them if they aren't here, right?

Here's the bottom line. You *can* help it that people aren't walking in the door. Maybe you shouldn't *have* to reach out and do a little personal marketing if you work for a large organization that is supposed to take care of that for you—but in the end, the results are yours. If people aren't walking in the door, get out your Rolodex. And maybe even your personal address book.

Picking up the reins

Back to Jennifer and her plight. When I talked to her about taking charge, I saw a door open. It was like watching her walk into a whole new, very large and beautiful room within her mind. I remember the moment it happened.

"You mean *I* could take charge, and do whatever it took to get people in the door?" she asked slowly.

"Exactly," I said. She thought a moment.

"Yeah, but they're supposed to do the marketing."

"Is it working?" I asked.

"No, but they might not want me out there doing this kind of thing."

"Maybe not. Check it out. They might be delighted," I said. "If I were your boss, I would be so excited about an employee taking that kind of initiative that I'd go to the ends of the earth to support them. But go ahead and ask them."

"Yeah, I will," she said. I could see the vision forming in her head. "Maybe I shouldn't have to do that, but it sure would be fun to raise the roof and get, like, totally outstanding stats that would knock them out."

I knew she was off and running. She bought a little guerrilla marketing book, but only read a few chapters. Once she began reaching out, she found that ideas occurred to her that would work even better than those in the book. People began to show up who had been standing next to her in line at the supermarket. Her friends began to appear, with *their* friends.

Jennifer got excited about her results and about gathering more and more people to the fitness center. Two months later, she called me to report that not only had her results become consistent, but they were up an average of 18%. Once she freed herself of the notion that she couldn't do anything if people weren't walking in the door, nothing could stop her.

"It was never gonna work, what I was doing," she told me. "I wanted sales, but I was leaning back to, you know, see what happened. It's easier just to go for it. Less stressed. If I need more people to walk in the door, I call people. This is like my mission, and I'm having fun. Oh, and my boss thinks I walk on water. I got a raise, and they want me to go around to all the other centers telling people what I do."

Opening that door changed Jennifer's life. She understands what it is to make a promise and know that she will keep it. She likes being the person her bosses go to for results, and she can call more shots at work now. Best of all, she's having more fun.

Jennifer embodies the generosity of spirit and the joy that are the essence of Step #6. It's not about being driven and miserable. When people "fall off the wagon" into misery, angst, or being driven, it's usually because they forget that they are in charge. Rather than taking action to create the result, they worry. Instead of picking up the phone, they sink into feeling pressured, strung out and stressed.

They begin to experience what I call the Three Nasty C's: complaint, crankiness and comfort-seeking. Not the positive, bubble-bath kind of comfort-seeking, but the insidious, diving-under-the-bed-to-mainline-chocolate kind of comfort-seeking—the kind we discussed in Chapter 4 on the Discomfort Dilemma. If you catch yourself engaging in any of these Three Nasty C's, it's time to stop and make a course correction. Take a deep breath and go to one of these "fixes."

THE STEP #6 "FIXES"

Step #6 is your chance to bring forth the hero within yourself. It is an act of heroism to keep going until you get the result. You overcome obstacles in your environment, and in your own mind. You face down the negative mental chatter and bring out the best in yourself. And you do it in the spirit of joy, generosity and grace. You are the contemporary mythic hero!

In every hero's journey, there are times when the odds seem impossible. Times when you feel as if you're hanging by your fingernails from a cliff. You just don't see how you can go on. For those moments, the Soul of Selling provides a toolbox full of "fixes." These "fixes" are designed to keep you out of trouble in the first place—but if you've already gotten into trouble, they will pull you back to safe ground. They will help you make course corrections, refocus on success, and rekindle your enthusiasm.

When you get to the end of your rope and don't think anything will get you to your promise, come to this chapter. Read over these "fixes" and choose one. If it doesn't work, choose another until you find one that *does* work. You can go through the entire list, or you can empower the first "fix" you choose. One way or another, your answer is here.

Fix #1: Start early, and keep going.

This is the Soul of Selling Motto. People often tell me it is the single most valuable tool they take from this approach. If you do nothing else, do this.

The root of many, if not most, problems in sales is that people don't start early enough. They wait until they are almost up against the date in their promise, and then panic and work under pressure. They try to take shortcuts, and get cranky when the shortcuts don't work. It's very difficult to access a spirit of generosity, compassion, or joy when you're working under the gun and feel as if you *must* get the result *now*. It's very hard to sell from this crimped-up energetic environment. Desperation is not attractive—and each time someone says "No," the situation becomes more desperate.

When you don't have a deadline looming over you, you can relax. You can be gracious. If somebody says "No," you can honor them and let them go. They're not out to ruin your statistics. *They're just not buying today*. You can take a deep breath, recreate the spirit of respect and generosity, and approach the next person with the same sense of appreciation.

Almost everybody has a nightmare experience that began when they started late. Sandy told me about the time that one of the chaperones for her son's school camping trip got sick and she had to take the kids to the woods for two days—but it was really three days by the time she got all the gear together, handled the food, and then got home and unpacked. These were exactly the three days, close to the date in her promise, that she had set aside to sell. She didn't keep her promise.

Helen told a story that demonstrated the other side of the coin. Her promise had been to recruit people to decorate for a community fund-raiser. She had a week to do it. Four days into the week, her mother passed away suddenly and Helen had to get on a plane to Indiana. It was a sad trip, but she didn't have to worry about the fundraiser because she'd made all her calls and kept her promise in the first two days.

The person with a death in her family kept her promise. The person with a camping trip didn't. Why? Because one started early, and the other didn't.

When you "Start early and keep going," selling is easier and more fun. It's no accident that I've listed it as the #1 Fix. If you do this, you are far less likely to need anything else.

Fix #2: Be willing to make course corrections.

How do you know when you need to make a course correction? When you're not getting the result. That's one reason promises are so valuable. They tell you when you are off course, so you can use them as truing mechanisms. You know in your gut when what you're doing isn't working, but here are some clear indications that it's time to make a course correction:

▶ You are three-fourths of the way through your allotted time and only one-fourth of the way through your results.
▶ You have just had five people in a row not buy because of the same objection.
▶ The conversation has gone south and your contact has become unresponsive.

These circumstances may seem like obvious clues that it's time for a course correction, but sometimes we become like deer stuck in the headlights. At the very moment when we need to see most clearly be-cause things aren't working, the fact that things aren't working makes us a little numb and throws us off our game. We aren't as perceptive or mentally quick as we normally are, and may not even consider the pos-sibility that we are off course.

We think it's other people's fault that we're not selling, or that the circumstances just aren't conducive to people buying. Or maybe the whole world is conspiring against us to produce a bad result, even though we're doing everything right. And we don't have *time* for course corrections. We can't stop now! We have a promise to keep! So we keep going 100 mph toward Mexico City, because we're already late for Seattle and can't be bothered to pause and recalibrate our course.

Course corrections are how we learn, how we grow, and what make the game interesting. But exactly what correction is needed? Fix #3 gives you some guidance about where to look.

Fix #3: Check the Course Correction Checklist.

If you don't know what isn't working, start here. The course correction you need may be on this list, or something here may prompt you to see what you need to do.

Course Correction Checklist:

1. *Have you done the first five steps?*
   ▶ Put down your baggage (and fix what you can).
   ▶ Pinpoint your passions.
   ▶ Create your Speaking Bank.
   ▶ Promise your result.
   ▶ Conduct the Ten-Touchstone Honoring Sales Conversation.
2. *Are you including all ten touchstones of the Honoring Sales Conversation?* Make sure you have:
   ▶ Seen people's value
   ▶ Made this value the foundation of your conversation, whether or not they buy. Are you irritated because people aren't buying? Is your attention on yourself, or on the other person?
   ▶ Connected with the other person. Are you in relationship with people before beginning your conversation?
   ▶ Shared your vision
   ▶ Found out the value to them of your product or service. What do they see in it for themselves?
   ▶ Invited them to participate
   ▶ Heard their objections without getting hooked. Are there any particular objections that are "sticking" around you? Any objections to which you feel particularly reactive?
   ▶ Taken them back to the value, if necessary
   ▶ Closed the sale. Are you seeing people as their best possible

selves and giving them a genuine choice, being willing to have people say "No" without withdrawing your appreciation?

▶ Validated their choice

3. *Are you being the adult in the conversation?* Are you the source of honor, respect and appreciation in this conversation? Or are you being reactive?

Fix #4: Create a Choice Chart.

It's stressful not to get a result. And under stress, sometimes we forget that we have choices about how we see things. The Choice Chart helps us remember.

First, make a list of your negative mental chatter in one column. This gets it out on the page, which is usually a great relief. Your list might look like this:

▶ I'll never make it now. I started too late.
▶ I just don't have what it takes.
▶ There aren't enough people to talk to for me to keep my promise.
▶ I hate this. It's degrading and humiliating and I'm going to fail.

Then, in another column, create an antidote for each piece of mental chatter. Make this a list of attitudes and beliefs that support your success. The corresponding list might look like:

▶ I just need to take a deep breath. Each time I talk to someone, I'm starting fresh.
▶ I like people and want to serve them, and that's all I have to do to succeed here.
▶ I'm willing to go find more people if need be, and I'll have fun doing it.
▶ This is a high calling, and I'm up to enjoying it and succeeding at it.

Then read over the second list without the first, and consciously choose to focus on that list.

Fix #5: Revisit your "value list" from Step #2.

In Step #2, you made a list of things you valued about selling, yourself as a seller, your product or service and your contacts. Use it. Read it over, print it up in a fancy font, or think of some other attractive way to keep it before you. Let these positive values fuel your enthusiasm and keep you going.

Fix #6: Use the Soul of Selling Chant.

If you have a pal who is also using the Soul of Selling, call that person up and whisper the chant together. Let it live in you. Truly, ask yourself if you want complaint or contribution? Drama or dreams? Struggle or service? Reasons or results? In the seminar, we all stand up and do a cheer based on the Soul of Selling Chant.

> Complaint to contribution, (arms up and to the left)
> Drama to dreams, (arms up and to the right)
> Struggle to service, (arms down and to the right)
> Reasons to results! (arms down and to the left)

(Repeat three times, then cheer and wave your arms above your head!)

Fix #7: Get a grip.

Years ago someone gave me a stand-up pillow doll about a foot high in the shape of a grim-looking dumpling woman. She's carrying a sign that says, "Snap out of it." We laughed, but I knew she was giving me a gentle reminder that I'd been going on about a particular "tragedy" for longer than was good for me.

When I need to get a grip with selling, I sometimes take out that pillow doll and put it on my desk. Just looking at her is usually enough to pull me out of the downward spiral. I listen to myself thinking, *Oh, I'm never going to keep this promise because I'm not having any fun, and I'm not having any fun because I'm not going to keep this promise....* I roll my eyes, and gently refocus.

The doll reminds me that I'm in charge, and that I can just as easily adopt another attitude. Instead of being swept away by the mental chatter, I can remember that all I'm really doing with these people is seeing the best in them. I'm just creating certainty and clarity in their lives and in mine. I'm finding out whether they're standing in the line of people who want to buy, or whether they're standing in the line of people who aren't going to buy but who are terrific anyway. That's all.

The pillow doll works for me. What works for you? What can you use to remind yourself to "Snap out of it" and get back on track when you feel that downward spiral overtaking you?

Fix #8: Create and use an Inspiration Bank.

Your Inspiration Bank is a collection of inspirational sayings, pictures, stories, quotes, symbols, tapes, books, or other items. Use it to keep your enthusiasm fresh, and renew it when it's flagging. These inspirational items may, or may not, be related to selling—but they pick you up and ignite your passion.

Fix #9: Create rewards.

Rewards are tremendously important. I don't care if it's a cabin cruiser or a gold star sticker on a stat sheet. Do what is reasonable for you and what makes you feel good. I went through a phase where I put glittery little red circle stickers around the margins of my stat sheet every time I got a sale. It reminded me of the little emblems that college football players put on their helmets. I got a kick out of it. That's what you're looking for. Something that jolts you out of your pattern and makes you think, *Hey! I did that! We are doing a great job!*

Set up a game. Each time you make a sale, give yourself a reward. It can be large or small, public or private, something you do by yourself or a group activity. Some sales teams come together for a cheer whenever anybody on the team makes a sale. Nothing that makes you feel good for succeeding is silly. Sometimes sillier is better. Figure out what makes you smile, then grab it and use it. Some of my favorite rewards are:

- ▶ Stickers on a sales chart (busy bees, red apples, gold stars, etc.)
- ▶ Going out to a nice lunch
- ▶ Calling friends or colleagues to cheer and spin the energy

What are your favorite rewards? What are some rewards you've never used before, but that might get you up and running? Develop a rewards bank from which you can pick and choose each time you keep a promise.

Fix #10: Revisit your heroism.

Remember that, as a seller, you are on a hero's journey *within* the hero's journey. You are learning lessons and developing your capacity to impact the world. You are evolving into your best self, and finding more meaning in life each day. You are operating out on the edge, connecting with the best in people. You are managing not only your own mental chatter, but also your contacts' mental chatter. You are holding the high watch, and being the one who ensures the integrity of the conversation, sees to people's needs, takes their hand and supports them through the process. You perform an alchemy that turns everybody's chatter into appreciation, respect, honor and gratitude—doing it all with ease and grace.

You keep moving every day into new levels of results, integrity, passion and ease—and you bring a lot of people with you.

Fix #11: Leave no room for failure.

The minute you entertain the possibility of not keeping your promise, you've opened a door that is hard to close. For the first few days after you make your promise, keep it as your primary focus. Start right away to keep it. If you need childcare, get it. If you need to clear more time than usual, clear it. Don't hope for the best. That's where failure starts.

Here's another pat-your-head-and-rub-your-stomach question: How do you leave no room for failure, but at the same time remain kind, optimistic and gentle with yourself? The first answer is: Practice. The next answer is: Start early. The next is: Use the "fixes" in this chapter as soon as you sense the need.

You can say, "no matter what," with a sense of dread, or with such hope, joy and optimism that the phrase becomes inspirational. It's not the words; it's the attitude behind the words. Six people could have six different attitudes toward "no matter what." These attitudes could range from fear, to grim determination, to anger, to hope, to certainty, to exultation. Make sure your attitude is inspirational.

Fix #12: Get support in doing these things.

Support is so important that I have devoted an entire chapter to it. You'll learn more in Chapter 12 about how to:

▶ Recognize when you need support.
▶ Determine what kind of support you need.
▶ Ask for it.
▶ Allow people to support you.

Fix #13: Remember the Big Rocks!

The Big Rocks Story is often told in business schools. It's a great reminder.

One day a professor told his class of business students, "Okay, time for a quiz." Then he pulled out a one-gallon, wide-mouthed mason jar and set it on the table in front of him. He took about a dozen fist-sized rocks and placed them carefully into the jar.

When the jar was filled with rocks, he asked, "Is this jar full?"

"Yes!" the class said.

"Really?" he asked. He reached under the table and pulled out a bucket of gravel. He dumped some gravel in and shook the jar, causing gravel to work itself down into the spaces between the rocks.

"Is the jar full?" he asked again.

"Probably not," they said cautiously.

"Good!" he replied, reaching under the table for a bucket of sand. He started dumping in the sand, which went into all the spaces left between the rocks and the gravel.

"Is this jar full?"

"No!" the class shouted.

"Good!"

He grabbed a pitcher of water and began to pour it in until the jar was filled to the brim. Then he asked the class, "What is the point of this illustration?"

One eager student raised his hand and said, "The point is, no matter how full your schedule is, if you try really hard, you can always fit some more things into it!"

"No," the professor responded, "that's not the point. The truth this illustration teaches us is: If you don't put the big rocks in first, you'll never get them in at all."

As with everything about the Soul of Selling, these "fixes" are meant to be modified and personalized to suit your specific situation and needs. Starting with the big things works for some people. Other people find it's better to start with one small task, and get it done. Which works best for you? Use whichever tactic suits your style. Remembering the Big Rocks simply means being aware of your options, and choosing what you know will work for you.

The capacity to keep going is the basis of your heroism. Use it to win, and to make each step richer than the last.

EXERCISES

EXERCISE #1: What are the three things most likely to stop you from keeping going until you get the result?

EXERCISE #2: What will you do as an antidote when each of these three things occurs?

PART 3

These chapters
show you
how to
take charge,
and how
to initiate and
support your
own enthusiasm,
joy and results.

TAKING CHARGE: BECOMING THE SOURCE OF YOUR OWN SUCCESS

CHAPTER 11

Mastery:
Owning Your Sales World

You've heard it a million times: Nobody succeeds in sales unless they are the source of their own success.

But how do you get there? How do you take charge of your life in sales, and move from hoping or struggling into mastery? How do you proceed with grace, poise, authority and ease to become a stand for your own success?

This chapter gives you tools to design your life in sales so that it serves you—and suggests ways to generate what you want with clarity, enthusiasm and appreciation.

WHERE ARE WE HEADED?

Before you start the journey, you need to know where you are going. In this chapter, you'll create a Personal Sales Vision. This Vision defines how you want your life in sales to be, and how you want each day to look and feel. It includes the physical and emotional environments that best serve your success, and the attitudes and personal strengths that you want to call forth and bring into your work.

You can't control everything in your sales world, but you can control what you bring to it. When you have that in place, you can put together a sales strategy for your individual situation, and create specific sales promises.

We all have different ideas of how we want our days to look and feel. Some people love the excitement of phones ringing off the wall, papers flying everywhere, techno-devices dripping from every fold of their clothing, and raucous, hail-fellow-well-met conversations demanding their attention from the minute they walk in the door until the minute they leave at night. Other people like a quiet office. You can actually see the surface of their desks, and phone calls are handled in an orderly and disciplined way. Still others don't like to go to the office at all. They prefer to sit in coffee shops, or even their cars, and sell by cell. Some people like to create a constant one-pointed focus on selling. Others like to break up their days with personal calls and intimate lunches.

None of these approaches is better or worse than any other. All are equally valid and effective *if that's what works for you.*

LAYING THE FOUNDATION

When you know what works for you, you can set up your days to galvanize your strengths, and to sidestep people and situations that deplete your energy. Lay your foundation with your Personal Sales Vision. This Vision has four parts:

1. Physical environment
2. Emotional environment
3. Organizational environment
4. Personal strengths that you want to call forth

YOUR PHYSICAL ENVIRONMENT

What do you want in your physical environment to support your success? This may seem trivial at first, but our physical surroundings impact how we feel and how we perform. The furniture, colors and other physical elements you have around you—and the way you arrange them—can keep your energy flowing cleanly and efficiently. Put more simply: if you like green and it makes you feel good, get some green around you.

No physical environment is perfect, but when things in your office or on your desk chronically don't work, they sap your energy. I sometimes let a pile accumulate on my desk that I mentally title "later," except all it does is keep growing. Each time I look at it, I get a little twinge. That one little twinge may not take much energy, but all the little twinges add up. They extract vitality that I could use to sell, or to strategize about selling—or even to go out to lunch, relax, and have a great time so that I return to work refreshed and ready to go.

Most of us have some limitations on our physical environment. I would prefer, for instance, to work on the beach in Hawaii with a temperature of seventy-two, sun in the sky, and a slight trade wind—but not enough to ruffle the papers on my desk, and no sand should get into any of my techno stuff. That's not realistic, meteorologically or financially, but there are some things in my environment I can control.

For instance, I like for my phone, lamp, pens and other items to be in certain places on my desk. I don't mind having little piles of papers around me on the floor for easy access. This would make other people crazy, but it works for me—especially since I work at home and nobody has to avoid rolling their desk chair over my little piles of paper. But it's not a good system when my neighbor's cat comes to visit. Her interpretation of the situation is that I've arranged a special play area for her—so when she's here, all that paper gets filed. Some people would roll their eyes at this system, but it works for me.

Twenty-five years ago, I spent $800 on a desk chair. It was a fortune for me then, but it resolved the back problems I was having and they haven't returned. I've had twenty-five years of sitting in a perfect chair for me, at about $.08 a day. The chair is still in perfect condition, and I'm in nearly perfect condition, so we could have another twenty-five years together. You tell me whether that was a good investment.

Those are just my preferences. Now let's look at yours. Check to see if you want to make any adjustments to your:

Desk:

▶ Does the placement of your phone, computer, lighting and other tools work for you?

▶ Does everything on your desk have a purpose? Photos and other items can have a purpose, or not. If a picture of your family, friends, or pets makes you feel good, keep it and maybe even get it blown up. If items are just sitting on your desk, taking up room and energy without contributing anything, think about removing them.

▶ Is your chair comfortable?

Computer:

▶ Is there anything that needs to be done to your computer to make it work for you? (Programs that need to be reinstalled? Keyboard need to be replaced? New mouse pad?)

Phone:

  ▸ Does your phone work for you? Does it feel good? Look good? Sound good? Or do you need another model?

  ▸ Do you have a headset? If you've been meaning to try a headset, do so now. For me, working without a headset is like writing with a quill pen. If you don't like the headset, you don't have to use it. But try it.

  ▸ Do you have the right amount of MHz or GHz in your cordless phone to allow a clear, clean connection with your contacts and also not interfere with anything else on your desk?

YOUR EMOTIONAL ENVIRONMENT

This may be the most important part of your Personal Sales Vision. How do you want to *feel* each day?

This is an area where you have some control. You can't control what comes into your environment, but you can control how you respond to it emotionally. You don't need to shut down any emotions that are less than saintly. We all have knee-jerk emotional reactions, every day—but you can learn to observe those knee-jerk reactions, and then look to see if that's what you want in your emotional environment.

For instance, Alice sold food supplements in a multi-level marketing program. When her down-line didn't produce good results, she got angry. "Some of them are actually scared of me and try to get out of my sight as quickly as they can," she told me. "Plus, I'm miserable. I don't like being angry and mean, and I beat myself up afterward. All the drama takes away from my results, and theirs."

Alice saw that she was creating an emotional environment that worked against her. At first, she didn't see how she had any control. "Hey, I'm angry," she said. "I can't just stop it, and it's no good trying to fake it, so what can I do?" It was a great question. She shouldn't try to fake it, but there was something she could do.

Alice didn't have to stuff the anger, but she could exercise some control over her emotional environment by "switching channels" to something else. In order to do that, she had to plan ahead. She knew that, in the midst of the anger, she wouldn't have the presence of mind to figure out what channel she wanted to watch instead. Her first thought was that she should shift her attention to the best in her down-line. That would have been ideal, but she very wisely saw that this was too big a shift, and simply not in her repertoire. She couldn't go directly from being angry with those people to being loving and compassionate toward them. She needed an interim step, a midway point between the two extremes where she could rest for a moment and recover her composure. Then, when she had cooled down a bit, she could shift to seeing the best in them.

For Alice, this neutral point was a painting that she loved. It hung above her desk, so when she was on the phone with people, she could actually look at it as she talked. When she was away from her desk, she could just hold that picture in her mind for a moment and let her emotions return to neutral. Then she could consciously call up thoughts of the best in her down-line. She saw them as people who were loved and who loved others, who wanted to contribute to life, and who had their own dreams and visions they wanted to achieve.

Part of being adults is that we gain some control over our emotions. Let these questions guide you through designing your own emotional environment:

▶ What do you want to feel as you approach each day?
▶ What kinds of interactions do you want to have with contacts?
▶ What do you want to think and feel about your team?
▶ What feeds you emotionally as you go about your day?
▶ When you get ready to leave at the end of the day, how do you want to feel about the job you've done?

Now let's look at how you want to set up your organizational environment.

YOUR ORGANIZATIONAL ENVIRONMENT

How do you organize your work? How do you manage your time? What structures work for you, and which don't work? Again, there are no right answers. The point is to get things organized in a way that works for you.

Here are some questions to ask yourself:

▶ How will you begin each day? Meditation? Meeting with the team? Making a "to do" list? All of these? In what order?
▶ What are the best times for you to call or see people? What are the best times to do paperwork and organizing? I am better first thing in the morning, so I do calls then. In the afternoon, when my energy tends to flag, I have times for paperwork and other activities that I can manage with "oatmeal brain."

- When will you make your promise for each day's results?
- What will your day look like as you move through it?
- What kind of lunch break is best for your energy? Some people like bringing food from home that they know they love. Others enjoy going to a restaurant.
- What helps you remember and organize your to do's? PDA? Some other system?
- Do you work with, or want to work with, a software program to organize your contacts and your interactions with them?

There is one more element in your Personal Sales Vision, and it is the most fun.

WHAT ARE YOUR STRENGTHS?

One of the most fulfilling elements of any job is bringing to it the things that you do particularly well. In Step #2, you pinpointed the unique strengths and skills that you bring to selling. Revisit those strengths, and add to the list if any more occur to you.

Answer these questions to call forth any more strengths and skills that you want to bring to your ideal day:

- What characteristics did you find that you valued most about yourself as a seller when you did Step #2?
- What other strengths do you have?
- What particular skills do you enjoy using when you sell?
- What qualities would you like to bring to work each day?
- What qualities do you think your team and contacts most appreciate about you? What qualities would they like to see more of?
- What qualities would *you* like to see more of?

Congratulations. You have all the elements you need to create your Personal Sales Vision. Now you can put them together into an inspirational tool.

CREATING YOUR VISION

Look over all your answers—physical, emotional, organizational and strengths. Underline the ones that are most important to you. As you bring together your Personal Sales Vision, focus on the emotional environment and on the strengths you want to bring. (For the most part, you can make changes in your physical and organizational environments without including them in your Vision—but if you want to include them, do so.)

Write one to three paragraphs that describe how you want each day to be for you. These paragraphs will be a touchstone, and you can revise them whenever you see something you'd like to add. Give yourself only about fifteen minutes to create your Personal Sales Vision. Don't think about it too much, and don't second-guess yourself.

Here are two samples:

Jed, St. Louis sporting goods sales manager: I begin each day by meeting with my team. We support each other, and that makes us enjoy the day more. We're working together, boosting each other up and celebrating each other's success. Customers like us and know they can trust us. We feel good about how we treat each customer. We send them out happy. We set goals we can make, and we make them. I'm a strong marketer, so I use that skill when we want more people in the store. I also make sure everybody's energy is up. We get together at the end of the day and talk about what we did. We handle any problems that come up and congratulate ourselves for a job well done. When I leave for the day, I feel like I've done the best job I could to sell our products and support my team.

Irina, day spa owner: Each morning when I open the blinds, I take a minute to soak up gratitude for having this business. I love this spa. I love how I've decorated it, and what I do with people here. I let my heart fill up with that, so that I can breathe it out to people all day long. Then I open the register, check the product displays, switch things around a little to wake up the energy, and review my Step #2 of what I value about the service I provide and the products I sell. As people come in, I honor and respect them. We have intimate interactions in which they are served. I focus on them. At the end of each day, I first tally up what I've sold and see if I made my promise for products. (I usually know who's coming each day, so I know how much I'll make on service. That is a separate thing.) Then I indulge myself in one of my services. I might give myself a facial, or even just sit enjoying one of the aromatherapy candles I sell. I close the blinds and leave with a feeling of satisfaction and accomplishment. I have a successful business that makes people more relaxed and beautiful. I am growing both my savings and my soul.

These Visions are overviews, big pictures, guidelines designed to shape your life in sales. They don't include every little bit of information you discover when you answer the questions, but they paint with broad strokes a picture of what you want your days to look and feel like. They put you in a much stronger position to be the source of what actually happens.

LETTING YOUR VISION SERVE YOU

What do you do with your Vision once you've created it? Don't let it sit idly on your hard drive, or in a file somewhere. Make it a living, breathing entity. Read it. Use it. See how quickly you can achieve everything in there, so that it's outdated and you have to create another Vision.

Jed read his Vision over coffee before he left for the office every morning. Irina made a tape of hers and listened to it on the way to work. Here are some other ways people have put their Visions to work for them:

- ▶ Read it before you get out of bed in the morning.
- ▶ Print out a beautiful copy and have it framed for your desk or wall.
- ▶ Keep it in a file on your desktop so you can peek at it from time to time during the day.
- ▶ Laminate a small version and keep it in your pocket or purse.
- ▶ When you meet with your team, each of you read your Visions to the group.
- ▶ Share your Vision with your spouse or partner so that he or she can support you.

Remember, your Vision is a work in progress. It must keep expanding as you do. One thing is certain in sales: You will change and grow. You won't be the same person next month as you are this month. You need a Personal Sales Vision that's up to speed with you, and that serves who you are today.

In the next chapter, we'll look at another vital part of taking charge of your life in sales—getting and allowing support from friends and colleagues.

EXERCISES

EXERCISE #1: If you have not already done so, answer the questions in this chapter and create your Personal Sales Vision.

EXERCISE #2: Make a list of the ways you can use your Vision so that it serves you most effectively.

CHAPTER 12

Generosity of Spirit:
Giving and Receiving Support

For "people people," many people who sell are notorious "Lone Rangers." Asking for support from the people in our lives—in the form of contacts, endorsements, time, money, referrals, enthusiasm, pep talks, foot massages, or just kind words on the phone—is uncomfortable for many of us.

People often ask me, "Does it count toward my promise if somebody helped me get the sale?" It's as if they had cheated if somebody supported them in keeping their promise. I try to shock them out of it by saying that it counts double. They are aghast!

The Soul of Selling asks a lot of us—a high level of service and personal interaction, making promises that we keep no matter what, even being adults! To work at this level, we need more than just our own energy. We need to learn to give and receive support.

Support is one of the most precious commodities on earth—and yet sometimes we don't even know what it would look like if somebody supported us. This chapter gives you tools to determine what kind of support you want, how to ask for it, and how to receive it. You will also discover how supporting and acknowledging others can build your own energy.

WHAT IS SUPPORT?

Support is anything that helps you do your job better or more easily. It can be physical, emotional, financial, intellectual, or energetic. The dictionary says that to support is "to actively promote the interests or cause of...to advocate, endorse...to provide means, force, or strength that is secondary; to give backup assistance to..."

Support is "secondary" and "backup." That means you can't turn over the reins to another person, and expect that person to do your job for you. That is abdication. Support occurs when you are ready and willing to do it all, but graciously and gratefully accept help when it is offered. You make sure the buck stops with you, but you also let people know that you are delighted and grateful to have their help.

Most people have more fun, and are more productive, when they make themselves part of a community of support. You may have many different kinds of support communities. You may have your gym pals, with whom you only exchange hellos but who are there each day at the same time you are, sweating away with you. Then there are your tennis or golf or basketball pals, or book club pals, or work pals, or movie pals. Often these people don't even know one another, but they are all important to you in some way. You may be intimate with some, and only say a few words to others. Yet they are all part of your network.

Support can take many forms. The ways people support you may have nothing to do with selling, something to do with selling, or everything to do with selling:

▶ You have lunch with an old friend from school, and hardly even talk about your jobs. But as you leave the restaurant, you know there is someone out there who cares about you, who wants you to succeed and whose buck is on you.

▶ You have lunch with an old friend from school, tell him what you're doing and collect a fistful of names and contacts along with a promise to call these people and recommend you.

▶ You have lunch with an old friend from school, and he becomes your biggest customer.

Support can also come from many directions:

▶ Your spouse might cook you an elegant dinner or take you out to a show.

▶ Your assistant might reorganize you so that you're better able to tell where you are with each contact.

▶ You might put together a group of friends who don't work together, but who have breakfast, lunch, or dinner once a week to "spin the energy" and buck one another up.

As with everything involved in selling, support is extremely personal. What makes your day could unmake another person's day—and vice versa. The important thing is to define what kind of support you want, and plan how best to get it.

THE CHALLENGE OF RECEIVING

I had a terrible case of the flu several years ago, and my neighbor called to ask if she could get me anything at the store.

"Oh no, I'm fine," I said instinctively, without even pausing to think whether I needed anything.

"Are you sure?" she asked. My silence must have tipped her off. "You do realize, don't you, that it would really make me feel good to bring you something? I'd feel like I was helping." I learned something important that morning. I saw that it really would make her feel good to help. I know it makes me feel good when I can help someone. I realized that I had often refused support when it was offered because I didn't want to put anybody out, or because I somehow thought "I'd owe them one."

When people are willing to support you, *let them*—especially if you've asked them to do it! It's one of the greatest gifts you can give people. It's a joy to give support. Be generous enough to let people be part of the win.

The higher the level at which we play, the more we need support. The Soul of Selling is a high-voltage endeavor that requires strong support. The good news is that most people particularly like supporting folks who are involved in high-voltage endeavors. It's exciting and juicy. They want some of it to rub off on them, and usually it does.

WHY WE RESIST SUPPORT
(AND HOW TO STICK YOUR TOE INTO THE POOL)

Why do we resist being supported? Here are some reasons people have given:

▶ I don't want to be beholden to anybody.
▶ I don't know what they might want in return.
▶ I'm embarrassed.

▸ I don't want them to think I'm needy.

▸ I don't want to appear weak or stupid.

▸ I need to prove I can do it myself.

▸ It'll give them power over me.

"Honestly, it's easier if I just do it myself," Howard told me. "The minute I get people around, depending on me, I have to spend all my time taking care of them."

Howard echoed what a lot of people fear about support. The assumption is that people are going to be troublesome, and that you will have to spend more time and energy taking care of them and fixing them than you would just doing the job yourself. Sometimes it turns out this way, but you can also set it up to work. First, let's look at how *not* to do it.

The Before Picture

Kate's insurance business had grown to the point that she hired two new people: one to manage the office and another to make "first contact" calls and qualify people for conversations with her. The office manager, Louise, had an ex-husband who kept showing up at the house and harassing her mother, who was taking care of her two kids. Louise had to leave and manage the situation, and then there were the lawyers and restraining orders, and the tears about money. Kate tried to help with salary advances, putting Louise in touch with various agencies, and being generous with personal time.

Cal, the "first contact" caller, wasn't really up to the job. He wasn't getting results, and Kate spent a lot of time trying to train him. But Cal obviously didn't like this kind of work, and made excuses for his lack of results.

Before Kate knew it, she was Big Momma and her insurance business was going to the dogs. She couldn't figure out what she was doing wrong. She rolled her eyes and told friends, "Just what I was afraid of. Having more people around is more trouble than it's worth."

But whose fault was it that the situation had deteriorated? Not Louise's or Cal's. They were just following their noses, trying to keep the walls from falling in. Kate needed to be clearer with Louise about what the job required. If Louise couldn't fulfill those responsibilities, she needed to find another job. Kate could be compassionate in communicating this, and even bend the rules a little if she wanted—but trying to fix Louise's life resulted in Louise's ex-husband holding the key to Kate's success or failure. She also needed to have a heart-to-heart with

Cal. Again, she could be compassionate and perhaps even help him find a job more suited to his skills and preferences—but to let him continue didn't support either of them.

The After Picture

Will also had concerns about support, but he took a different path. He was a life coach who saw that support could enhance his practice, but he had always been a loner. He had shied away from support because he thought it would make him indebted to other people. Then he would have even more to do. He was willing to experiment, however, and the results shocked him.

Will put his toe into the water by asking his wife, Tara, for support. He asked her to call him once each morning and once each afternoon. She was a medical technician with a busy schedule, but she was flattered and delighted that he had asked her. She had always wanted to support him in some way, but didn't know what he wanted or needed. Rather than tackling what she rightly interpreted as his resistance to support, she had left him alone.

The calls were great fun for both of them. She said, "It feels like we're dating again." He loved the attention, and she was delighted when he told her how much they picked up his day.

Pleased with this result, Will stepped out a bit more. He invited some friends to lunch, other people who had their own businesses and wanted to expand what they were doing. He made a point of engaging them in talk about what was working for them in their practices. The lunch was a big success. All four men left enthusiastic and ready to take on the world. Two of them called Will that afternoon to thank him, and they decided to meet once a month, just to remind one another of what was possible in their profession, and to open a window on the positive for one another.

These weren't big things, but more people started calling Will about coaching. Some were referrals from his lunch buddies, or friends of friends of people they had told about Will's coaching practice. He had also done some outreach and followed up on some ideas suggested at the lunch group. Within three months, Will had more clients, was making more money, and was doing more of what he loved to do. "I feel like a better guy," he told me, "at home, with my colleagues, and with my clients. I'm glad I gave it a try."

Whether you are just starting out and want to attract clients, or your business is successful and you want to take it up a notch, getting support can enhance both the quantity and the quality of your sales.

Begin by knowing what kind of support you want, from whom you want it, and how to ask for it.

WHAT KIND OF SUPPORT DO YOU WANT?

Each of us needs and wants different kinds of support. All the various types of support—professional, emotional, physical, financial, intellectual and energetic—tend to merge into one another, but here are some common ways that people like to be supported. Read over the list and see which appeal to you:

Professional
- ▶ Suggestions for contacts
- ▶ Ideas for marketing
- ▶ Advice about selling in general, and about educational programs
- ▶ Information about office space, or deals on equipment
- ▶ Names of people for staff
- ▶ People whom they would call to recommend or endorse you

Emotional
- ▶ Calls or cards saying they support you
- ▶ Smiles
- ▶ Footrubs, backrubs, etc.
- ▶ Hearing "You're terrific" or "I love you"

Physical
- ▶ Keeping your desk neat
- ▶ Handling your phone calls professionally and in an inviting way
- ▶ Setting up your scheduling system or PDA so that it works for you
- ▶ Researching a desk chair

Financial
- ▶ Giving you "seed money"
- ▶ Buying from you
- ▶ Recommending investors, clients, or contacts

Intellectual
- ▶ Referring you to articles or books that support you
- ▶ Discussing the business and giving input
- ▶ Talking about new ideas or markets for your business

Energetic
- ▶ Just being on your side
- ▶ Pep talks
- ▶ Generating enthusiasm for your job or project

The things that would best support you may not even be on this list. Take a moment to see what would make your job easier. What would grease the wheels of your success? What would genuinely help?

WHO CAN GIVE IT?

Support can come from anywhere. The more open you are, the more possibilities are available to you. Beth was a financial advisor who wanted to get back into shape and made an appointment with Charlotte, a physical trainer. They started talking during Beth's session, and ended up referring clients to one another.

Be open to support from anyone, but start with this list of people from whom you might particularly enjoy it:

- ▶ *Your team at work.* Look up, down and sideways for this kind of support. What could your boss do to support you? What could people who report to you do? Your peers? When you succeed, all of these people succeed. You may be surprised at how eager they are to support you, once they know what you really want.
- ▶ *Your family.* Your spouse, kids, siblings and parents can be wonderful sources of support. If these people knew what they could do to support you, they would probably jump at the chance to help. (Wouldn't you want to support *them*?) And they will probably be very flattered that you asked.
- ▶ *Your friends.* If you feel comfortable with this, it's a great way to extend your friendships into your professional life. What could your friends do to support you in selling? What about old friends you haven't see for a while? What would you like to do to support *them*? Have you ever asked them how you could support them?
- ▶ *Your professional associates.* Do you belong to an association? What are some new ways for you and your colleagues to support one another?
- ▶ *Who else?* Take a moment to think of anyone else in your life whose support you would like to have, and what form that support would take.

ASKING FOR SUPPORT

Sometimes we don't ask for support because we don't know how to do it. We don't want to impose, or put people on the spot. We know that we like supporting other people, and have a sense that others would like to support us, but asking for support can feel sticky.

The bottom line is this: To attract the kind of support you want, be the kind of person *you* would want to support. Ask yourself, *What would I want to know, or to hear, if I were in this person's shoes and they were asking me for support?*

Here are some guidelines for asking for support:

1. Be clear about what you want.

Know exactly what you want from people before you ask them. Don't approach people with, "Hey, I could use some, you know, help. What do you, like, you know, think you might be able to do to support me?" That will most likely produce confusion, frustration, and/or resentment, rather than support. Instead, take some time to think about what you really want and to develop your request:

▸ Anne, I'd love to have your support. Would you be willing to sit with me for an hour and talk about people you think I should approach?

▸ Gerry, I'd like to take you to lunch and pick your brain about contacts. I'd be happy to have you pick my brain, too, if you'd like.

2. Be very specific in your requests.

Whether the support is personal or professional, vague requests make people nervous. Understandably so. A blanket promise for "support" can mean anything from buying the person a cup of coffee to fostering their firstborn child. The more vague your request, the less likely they are to agree—and the less fulfillment they will feel, even if they do go out on a limb.

When the request is clear and specific, people can make good choices about whether or not they can help—and feel a sense of accomplishment when they give it to you. Here are some examples of clear, specific requests:

▸ Thanks for asking what you could do, Bill. It would be a huge help if you could research this list of contacts. I need names, positions, full contact information and their history with us over the past five years.

▶ Honey, I love your calls. Would you mind if we talked in the afternoon rather than the morning? That's when I get a little slow, and I'd love to have your support then. Could we make it sometime between three and four o'clock?

3. Ask directly. Don't beat around the bush.

Have you ever had someone call you, and then hem and haw about making their request? It's as if they didn't know how to ask, or didn't know what to ask for (and wanted you to figure it out), or were afraid to ask at all, or assumed you wouldn't want to help them out, or didn't think they were worthy of being supported. All these things can put people off. Anything less than a straightforward request can make people feel as if they are being manipulated in some way. It's easier to support people who ask for specific support in a clear and "straight from the shoulder" way.

▶ Helen, I have a favor to ask of you. Can we have lunch next week to talk about specific ways we can support one another?

▶ Joe, it seems to me that our businesses are complimentary, and that we might be able to refer our clients back and forth. Would you be willing to meet to talk about it?

▶ Sweetheart, I know you're busy, but remember last year when you left those little notes in places where I'd just stumble across them? I loved that and I could use a little extra support right now. Could you do that again, please?

4. Make your request an invitation, rather than a plea for help without which you will probably go under (and it will be their fault!).

It's attractive to support people who don't necessarily need you, but who want you to participate with them. Adopt this attitude with the people whom you are asking for support. Be sure they know that it's okay to say "No," and that your relationship with them won't suffer if they aren't able to support you. You'd love to have them on board, but you understand if they are too busy or just don't want to do what you ask.

▶ John, please be straight with me if this doesn't work for you, but I'm getting together a group of people Friday who may be willing to support my new business with ideas, contacts, or just good wishes. I want to invite you. It's fine if you can't come, but I'd love to have you there.

5. Be grateful—out loud, and in a way they appreciate.

Be specific about what they've done to help you, and about the difference it has made for you.

- ▶ Thanks for the call, Karen. It was just the pick-me-up I needed and I appreciate your support very much. I did a better job because of it.
- ▶ Allen, I so appreciate the way you organized my calls today. It was "above and beyond," and that's what makes us a great successful team.
- ▶ Sue, thanks for sending the "I believe in you" card. I'm grateful that you're my pal.
- ▶ Honey, the backrub this morning is the total reason I met my goal today. I love you, and I want to take you out to dinner.

When people help you succeed, make a point of telling them how much you appreciate what they did. Let them know the specific ways they made your job easier or more productive. Make your acknowledgment public, if it's possible and appropriate.

GIVING SUPPORT

Most of us have less trouble giving support than we do receiving it. We want to help, and can always find some way to make life easier or more enjoyable for other people. It's important to keep this natural generosity of spirit alive, even in the midst of our promises and busyness. Be the eye of the hurricane, the island of generosity that people can trust even when everyone else is going crazy.

Here are some ways to support others that relate specifically to the Soul of Selling:

- ▶ *See the best in people.* Whatever your interaction with them—selling, lunch, playing cards, socializing—remember to respect, honor and appreciate them. Even if you say or do nothing, they will feel how you are seeing them—and they will blossom.
- ▶ *Demonstrate this respect, honor and appreciation.* You might comment on something they did, or some way they interacted with people, that showed some personal quality that you admire. You might send them a card or email saying how much you appreciate them, and note something specific they said or did.
- ▶ *Stay connected with people when you speak with them.* Be generous

with your attention. Don't let your mind wander, even if you have a lot to do. You will probably be the person who heard them most fully and clearly that day.

▶ *Be interested, rather than interesting.* Put your attention on them. Shift your focus from your own problems, to what you can do to support and contribute to them.

ACKNOWLEDGMENT

Acknowledgment is the backbone of the Soul of Selling. It's what keeps us strong, and helps us remember who we are and what we are doing. True acknowledgment is different from compliments. Compliments tend to deal with externals and appearances. Acknowledgments tend to be about internal qualities you admire, and how you noticed that people demonstrated those qualities.

Compliments:

▶ I love your hair, Joan.
▶ Great suit, Ted.
▶ You guys have terrific offices.

Acknowledgments:

▶ I know you had to go beyond where you thought you could go to get those results, Andy. Congratulations.
▶ You were very courageous in that situation, Ed.
▶ Your interaction with her was very compassionate, Doris.

There's nothing wrong with compliments. They feel good, too. There are times when I would much rather have somebody say they like my hair than that I was compassionate. But acknowledgment goes to a deeper level. You are saying that you saw part of who the other person is, and that you appreciate the opportunity to be present to that.

Acknowledgment is often the very best support you can give someone. Acknowledging others for their support of you makes them feel good, but it makes you feel even better. It's like walking around with $1,000 bills in your pocket, giving them away from an endless supply. It takes nothing away from you, and gives people something that they cherish. It's free to you, and incredibly valuable to them.

EXERCISES

These exercises will give you a support plan. You'll make five lists. When you have these lists, all you have to do is follow the dots:

EXERCISE #1: What are some ways that people can support you?

EXERCISE #2: Who could provide this support?

EXERCISE #3: When will you ask them?

EXERCISE #4: What might be in the way of receiving this support?

EXERCISE #5: What can you do to move beyond this and accept the support?

CHAPTER 13

The Soul of Selling as Personal Growth:
Becoming the Person You've Always Wanted to Be

I originally developed the six steps of the Soul of Selling for myself, as a way to use selling as a vehicle for personal growth. In order to stay sane, happy, fulfilled and successful over a thirty-year career in sales, I needed a way to make selling not only fun, but also a source of spiritual enrichment.

The Soul of Selling tagline is "Whether you want enlightenment or just fistfuls of money—or both—selling will get you there." This chapter shows you how to ensure that you get exactly the personal benefits you want most from selling. You will define those benefits, and plan how to use the Soul of Selling to get them. This is your "value added" chapter.

THE SPIRITUAL DOUBLE WHAMMY

Selling is a cornucopia of lessons. Hardly a moment passes without an opportunity to live with more compassion, more generosity, and more personal clarity and strength. When you look for these opportunities, you grow personally and spiritually, as well as professionally. You enjoy the worldly success of great results in sales, and also the spiritual success of growing into the person you have always wanted to be.

As you grow, you take all that you've learned out into every other aspect of your life. The compassion you master while conducting the Honoring Sales Conversation can enrich your relationships with your parents, your kids, your friends, or your colleagues. Learning to keep going until you get the result can help you persevere with wallpapering, putting up new kitchen cabinets, getting your taxes done on time—or with saving a marriage, or surviving your children's teen years. Learning to close sales and bring people to a point of choice can translate into "closing" a vacation to the Bahamas or selling a house.

THE SOUL OF SELLING AS SPIRITUAL PRACTICE

I know many people who are spiritual seekers, and who look down their noses at people who sell. It's all I can do to keep from saying, "Forget the mountaintop. Get a job selling cars, and you'll be enlightened in half the time!"

The Soul of Selling actually parallels many approaches to personal growth and spiritual practice. Most spiritual practices include four principles:

▶ Quieting the mind
▶ Equanimity
▶ Balance of love and will, yin and yang, compassion and power
▶ Service

Here is how these four principles work in the Soul of Selling:

▶ *Quieting the mind.* It asks you to manage mental chatter, and also to be compassionate with your contacts' mental chatter. You are no longer a slave to mental chatter; you become senior to it in order to contribute. You identify and release your own mental chatter before the interaction—and learn to hear buyers' chatter without necessarily believing it. The capacity to rise above mental chatter gives you access to levels of strength and compassion that are simply not possible when you run after every thought in your mind—and other people's minds.
▶ *Equanimity.* It teaches you to be the eye of the hurricane. Selling is demanding business. Yet in the midst of everything, you remain compassionate, committed and calm. You are a grown-up who is willing to make the whole experience rich for everyone involved—and to have everybody win.

▶ *Balance.* It demands an amalgam of love and strength, generosity of spirit and steady will, humility and certainty, yin and yang. It asks that you guarantee two things that many people believe are mutually exclusive: 1) Guaranteeing specific results, and 2) Unconditional honoring and appreciation of your contacts. You bring yourself up to the best you have to offer people. Your ego isn't so fragile that you are thrown off track by hearing "No." You are willing to see beyond people's crankiness, uncertainty, or defensiveness to the goodness in them. At the same time, you produce the promised result, every time. You merge personal effectiveness with contribution, and powerful results with personal meaning.

▶ *Service.* It is based on service. The Soul of Selling always calls you to new levels of service. Your primary charge is to see the best in people, to see them as they really are. This is the greatest service one human being can offer another. You make that the foundation of your relationship and learn to recognize and dismantle everything that might get in the way of that service.

THE SIX STEPS AS SPIRITUAL PRACTICE

Each of the six steps brings its own form of spiritual practice. Beyond each step's obvious application to selling, here is how it promotes spiritual and personal growth:

1. *Put down your baggage (and fix what you can).* You unearth beliefs that limit your ability to be compassionate, expansive, generous and powerful in the world—and then put them aside so that you can serve each person with whom you interact, and bring your vision into the world.

2. *Pinpoint your passions in selling, in yourself as a seller, in your product or service, and in your contacts.* You build a platform of authentic, clearly defined, and often spiritual values from which to launch everything you do. You can return to these values for inspiration and guidance whenever you feel less than fully engaged or spiritually enriched.

3. *Create your Speaking Bank.* You learn to speak about what you value in an inspiring way, and to frame what you say so that it serves and enlivens people. You develop your capacity to engage and support the best in people.

4. *Promise your result.* You take a stand for your results, which trans-

lates into taking a stand for what you value, for contributing to others, and for yourself. You go beyond good thoughts and positive talk; you guarantee results that make a difference. The capacity to do this changes your life, because you can move visions from the realm of thoughts into physical reality, where they can contribute to people. You can be the "go to" person in your family, your community, or wherever you want to serve.

5. *Conduct the Ten-Touchstone Honoring Sales Conversation.* You know how to conduct a conversation that is guaranteed to serve others in the most fundamental way, by seeing the best in them and holding that vision regardless of what they say or do. You can translate this capacity to conversations with friends, family, strangers and the world.

6. *Keep going until you get the result.* You are not just sitting on the sidelines of life, thinking good thoughts and hoping for the best. You get the result, every time—in sales and in life. To keep going, you need faith, trust, integrity, passion and the ability to re-ignite all these things at will. These are skills that will get you through anything from a Dark Night of the Soul, to challenging personal situations, to looking courageously and directly at what you are here on Earth to do and making sure it happens.

As you practice the six steps over and over, these spiritual practices become part of how you live your life.

SELLING PARAGONS

I am inspired by people who use the Soul of Selling as a spiritual practice to become the people they always hoped to be. Here are two of their stories:

Keeping a Promise

My friend Ted wasn't interested in spiritual matters, but he wanted to be a bigger, better, deeper or more effective person. Ted is charming and brilliant. He never had to work very hard to succeed, and so he never set goals or made promises. He just followed his nose, and things usually worked out well for him. When he began using the Soul of Selling, he decided to milk it for all it was worth. He wanted to go for the added value.

Ted didn't like the whole idea of making promises, but he was willing to do it—and to use it to make his life richer. He discovered that he actually enjoyed making promises and keeping them. "It's a bigger deal when I've actually promised something and made it happen. I don't feel so much like it's just good luck. I have a real sense of accomplishment and achievement."

Ted became the promise king, and began making and keeping promises in his personal life as well. Instead of hanging out and just seeing what happened with his Saturdays, he made promises to wash the car, take the kids to the movies, work out, or finish a woodworking project. His initial resistance to "giving up my day off, when I can just hang out" turned into appreciation for the pleasure he got from being with his kids, feeling good physically and completing projects.

"I could have just wasted those days in front of the TV," he said. "I know what I'm doing now, and I don't have that 'drifty' feeling. I'm choosing my life, getting more done, and doing more things I like," he said. Needless to say, his wife, Beth, was just as happy as he was.

Warming Up

Shelly sold medical supplies, and at first she had a tough time seeing the best in every person she contacted. She was a no-nonsense person who liked to stick to business and deal in facts. She approached what she called "the warming up process" of the Soul of Selling with some trepidation, but with a great deal of determination. She set up a system whereby before each interaction with contacts, she actually sat down and read a list of qualities that she was willing to respect, appreciate and honor in them.

Over the months, she grew to enjoy the warmth and authenticity of her connections with people. She decided that she wanted to be more open, and a little softer, with friends and family as well. She wanted to let the appreciation and respect for others that she had cultivated while using the Soul of Selling "warm up" her personal life. Again, she set up a system. Once a week, she had someone over for dinner. These little dinners became very popular, and everybody wanted to be the one who was invited that week. Gradually, they grew into larger dinner parties and Shelly's personal life became far richer and more expansive than it had been.

"Sometimes I can't believe this is me," she told me at lunch. "But life is much more fun this way. When I look back, I can't even believe I ever thought it was hard."

Value Added

Ted and Shelly both looked at what "added value" they wanted from the Soul of Selling, and intentionally let the skills they learned and the qualities they cultivated carry over into their personal lives.

Other people have learned different skills using the Soul of Selling, and transferred into their personal lives their newfound capacities to:

▶ Be a stand for their own success, as a result of keeping promises "no matter what."

▶ Appreciate, respect and honor other people, even if they had to "fake it 'til you make it."

▶ Go beyond where they had gone before in producing results, and beyond where they thought they could go.

▶ Overcome discomfort and crankiness to produce a result that made them happy.

YOUR OWN "ADDED VALUE"

Your "added value" comes more quickly, thoroughly and easily if you know what you want.

"Subtracted" attitudes

Let's look first at things you want to improve. Many of us are aware of negative attitudes, beliefs, opinions, behaviors and fears that hold us back in selling. These attitudes may get in our way in other aspects of life as well. What are some attitudes or behaviors that you would like to move beyond, in selling and in life?

Here are some answers people have given:

▶ I don't think I'm worthy of success.

▶ I'm afraid of failing, so I don't give it my all.

▶ I don't want to be the adult, the one in charge of people feeling good about themselves.

▶ I procrastinate, and put everything off until the last minute.

▶ I drive myself too fast, and then don't have as much fun.

▶ I start out well, but then lose steam and don't know how to re-energize myself.

Where are we going?

What parts of yourself do you want to nurture through selling, and transfer into the rest of your life? What are some attitudes, skills and behaviors that you want to strengthen?

Here are some examples:

▶ I want to feel in charge of my life, and give up this victim stuff.
▶ I want to be a person who genuinely likes people.
▶ I want to be a powerful person who says what they are going to do, and does it.

Who do you want to be?

"The person you've always wanted to be" needs some definition. The clearer you are about who you want to be, the more likely you are to become that person. What does the person you've always wanted to be look like?

These are some answers people have given:

▶ I want to be someone to whom people look for guidance, support and nurturing.
▶ I want to be strong, to know that I can do the things I want in life without a lot of effort or drama.
▶ I want to be a results person rather than a couch potato, but I want to do that in a way that's relaxed and graceful.
▶ I want to be a person who sees the best in everyone, and around whom people just feel good.

THE SELLER WHO CHANGED THE WORLD

My personal inspiration for selling is Mother Teresa. She had a vision based on authentic personal values, and overcame everything in the way of realizing that vision. She discovered how to energize her resources and speak effectively to people about giving her money to help the poor. She saw everyone she contacted as the Christ, and she kept going until she got the result. That is compassion, combined with clarity and commitment, in service to others. That is spiritual practice.

What if Mother Teresa had just sympathized with the poor of Calcutta? What if she had felt very sad about them and talked about them with her friends over lattés, but rejected any real action because the scope of the problem was so large? Or because going around asking people for money wasn't "spiritual"? Or because she didn't want to rock the boat and question the system? Or because she might be uncomfortable, embarrassed, or rejected?

Instead, Mother Teresa became a force of nature. She sold her vision, raised a great deal of money, and made the world a better place because she was in it. You can do those same things, on as large a scale as you please.

Congratulations. You have taken some huge steps. The Soul of Selling can give you more than success; it can give you the life you've always wanted to live. All you need to do now is get out there and use these principles. Give them your all, and they will give you back more than you can possibly imagine.

EXERCISES

EXERCISE #1: Answer these questions:
- ▶ What do you want the Soul of Selling to do for you, professionally and personally?
- ▶ What do you want to release as a result of using this method?
- ▶ What qualities or skills do you want to bring forward?
- ▶ Who is the person you want to be?

CHAPTER 14

Your Soul of Selling Synergy Group

A Soul of Selling Synergy Group can keep your spirit agile and your enthusiasm vibrant. It can keep you on track with your promises, and give you and your colleagues a place to support one another, exchange ideas, and use the Soul of Selling for all its worth.

WHAT DOES A SYNERGY GROUP LOOK LIKE?

Most Synergy Groups form within companies, and are made up of people who sell together and work toward common goals. However, you can just as easily put together a Synergy Group with friends or colleagues outside your business. I recommend you keep the size of the group between two and ten, but I have seen larger groups work very well.

Synergy means that the whole is greater than the sum of its parts. The energy you and your colleagues generate is greater than if you just added up Jen's energy, Rick's energy and Don's energy. You create among you a greater force from which you can all draw. You can think of this force as information, as experience or expertise, as support, or simply as energy. The point is that you come together so that each of you can get more personal and professional benefit from the Soul of Selling.

Most groups meet every week or every two weeks, but you can get together more often at first if you wish. The format suggested in this chapter works well, but you can use any format that supports your group.

WHAT DOES IT DO?

The purpose of a Synergy Group is to support each member in using The Soul of Selling. Your group is a place to:

▶ Deepen your understanding of how the Soul of Selling works
▶ Practice each step fully and with the support of the group
▶ Share information and experiences
▶ Synergize your energy so that everyone takes their results to the next level
▶ Provide support for people to keep going and win

If your group is working, you should all be selling more and enjoying it more.

THE SYNERGY GROUP FORMAT

Basically, you will focus on one chapter of this book at each meeting. You'll discuss it, bring your own ideas and suggestions to it, and then take it out into your selling worlds and test-drive it. You'll come back to the next meeting with experiences to share, ideas about how to get the most benefit, stories about what worked and didn't work, and general enrichment for your group.

When you've gone all the way through the book, you can start again or find another format that works for you. You will find that, after thirteen chapters and thirteen weeks, you are all in a different place than you were when you started. That means you will get something entirely different from the chapters than you did the first time around.

How does it work? Let's start with the first meeting, which is a little different from subsequent meetings.

Your First Meeting

As the person who got the group together, begin by welcoming people and thanking them for coming. Then you can follow this outline, or create another that may work better for your group.

1. *Welcome.* Let people know that you appreciate their taking the time to come and find out about the group.
2. *Agenda.* Tell people what will happen at this meeting. Let them know what time the meeting will end. If you have water, coffee, or snacks, invite them to partake.
3. *What is a Synergy Group?* Tell them about the group and its pur-

pose, using this chapter as a guide. Be sure to mention what they can hope to gain from being part of it, that each meeting will focus on a different chapter of this book, and that between meetings they will have exercises and assignments designed for them to get the most possible benefits from using the Soul of Selling.

4. *Explain the format.* Let them know that tonight is different, but that there is a format that the group will follow each week. It's not set in stone, but you'll be starting with the format described later in this chapter.

5. *Introductions.* Ask each person to share their name, what they sell, how they came to be there and what they would want to get out of being part of the Synergy Group.

6. *Sharing.* You or someone in the group can share the benefits you've received from the book, and tell your personal reasons for wanting to form the group.

7. *Invite their questions or sharing.* What do they see for themselves about what you have said? Where are they now? Where do they want to be with selling? Do they have any questions?

8. *What would they like to get out of the group?* Give people a chance to add their ideas.

9. *Group decisions*:
    i. *Chair.* You can elect a chair, or appoint/volunteer a new chair for each week.
    ii. *Frequency.* How often do you want to meet?
    iii. *Location.* Where?
    iv. *Time.* What time, and for how long will you meet?

10. *Agreements.* I suggest that people make the agreement to come to each meeting, to be on time, and to have read the assigned chapter.

11. *For next meeting*:
    i. When is it?
    ii. Read Chapter 1 of this book. Make a note of any questions you have, or anything you'd like to share or discuss.

I suggest you find out who is coming to the next meeting, so you can anticipate how many people will be there for setup and/or refreshments.

Regular Meetings

This is a format that has worked for many groups. You may want to start with this, and modify it over time to suit your group's particular needs.

1. *Welcome.*
2. *Check-in.* Everybody says hello and tells the group one thing they appreciated about their day. This is to get people present and connected.
3. *Sharing* since the last meeting:
   i.   What did you notice about how the chapter played out in your life and work?
   ii. What did you notice as you practiced the Soul of Selling principles?
4. *Promises.* Reports on whether or not people kept their promises. This is just a "Yes" or "No" without explanations or excuses.
5. *Questions or challenges* since the last meeting that people want to bring to the group for suggestions or discussion. This could also involve asking for some coaching if they didn't keep their promises.
6. *Summary of the chapter* under discussion. (Everyone will have read this new chapter, but one person can spend about three minutes summarizing it.)
7. *Discussion of the chapter.* You can use the Discussion Questions in this chapter, or come up with your own. It's important to point out that there are no right answers to these questions. Their purpose is simply to stimulate discussion. They should not be treated as a quiz.
8. *Practicing the principles.* People share what principles from this chapter they want to focus on between this meeting and the next. It could be seeing people as their best selves, keeping the attention on others, remembering their own strengths as a seller, etc.
9. *Promises for next meeting.* Everybody makes a sales promise that they will keep before the next meeting.
10. *For the next meeting:* Remind people what chapter to read for the next meeting.
11. *Inspiration.* At each meeting, someone brings an inspirational reading or story to share. After the Inspiration is given, select someone to bring it next time.
12. *Adjourn.*

DISCUSSION QUESTIONS

Here are some questions to kick off discussions of each chapter. Use these, let them prompt other questions, or come up with entirely new questions. The point is for people to use the material as fully as possible, for them to make it work in their own situations, and for them to "own" it.

Discussion Questions for Chapter 1

▸ What is the difference between "selling" the Soul of Selling way, and selling as you knew it before?
▸ What does "soul" mean for you?
▸ What do you see as the particular advantages to you of the Soul of Selling?
▸ What do you see as your challenges with this method?
▸ What do you "sell" in life, other than your product or service?

Discussion Questions for Chapter 2

▸ Do you see a flow to the six steps? How does each one lead to the next?
▸ How do you see each step working in your particular situation?

Discussion Questions for Chapter 3

▸ Which of the internal and external advantages interest you most?
▸ Which skills interest you?
▸ Which of the things that the Soul of Selling costs you seemed either interesting or daunting to you? Why?
▸ What did you see when you did the Exercises for this chapter?

Discussion Questions for Chapter 4

▸ Where does the Discomfort Dilemma show up in your life?
▸ What does your mental chatter sound like when you hit the Discomfort Dilemma?
▸ What are some antidotes you discovered?
▸ What did you see when you did the Exercises for this chapter?

Discussion Questions for Chapter 5

▸ Have you ever experienced a disappointing result from carrying around baggage? If so, what happened?
▸ Did you work through the checkpoints? If so, what happened?

- What did you discover when you practiced switching channels?
- What did you discover working Step #1 that you didn't know before?
- What did you see when you did the Exercises for this chapter?

Discussion Questions for Chapter 6

- What was your favorite value or passion in each area?
  - Selling in general
  - Yourself as a seller
  - Your product or service
  - Your contacts
- What were five values you were willing to see in your contacts?
- What did you see when you did the Exercises for this chapter?

Discussion Questions for Chapter 7

- What is your larger Vision?
- What is your first ten-second sound bite?
- Have you practiced in the mirror or on video?
- Give us the highlights of your Speaking Bank.
- What did you see when you did the Exercises for this chapter?

Discussion Questions for Chapter 8

- What are all your "Yeah, buts" for making promises?
- What are the three top things that you want making promises and keeping them to do for you?
- What are your complaints? Your contribution? Your drama? Your dreams? Your struggle? Your service? Your reasons? Your results?
- What did you see when you did the Exercises for this chapter?

Discussion Questions for Chapter 9

- Which of the ten touchstones in the Honoring Sales Conversation are you already doing as a matter of course?
- Which are you not doing?
- What values do you see in most people?
- Have you test-driven the Honoring Sales Conversation? What did you discover? Did you particularly enjoy any specific part of it? Was there any part that was challenging?
- What did you see when you did the Exercises for this chapter?

Discussion Questions for Chapter 10

▸ What do you see about the hero's journey within the hero's journey? What does that mean to you?

▸ Who is the Donut Man in your life? Is there anyone who inspires you with their spirit of generosity and contribution?

▸ Have you ever given up on a result? How did it feel? What could you have done, knowing what you know now and using the Soul of Selling, to guide that situation to a better result?

▸ What excuses are you inclined to use?

▸ Which of the "fixes" do you think will be most useful to you?

▸ What did you see when you did the Exercises for this chapter?

Discussion Questions for Chapter 11

▸ What is your Personal Sales Vision?

▸ What is your emotional environment like now?

▸ What strengths will you be bringing to selling?

▸ What did you see when you did the Exercises for this chapter?

Discussion Questions for Chapter 12

▸ Who in your life most clearly embodies generosity of spirit?

▸ Who supports you at work? In life? What does that support look like?

▸ Whom do you support at work? In life? What does that support look like?

▸ What did you identify as areas in which you want more support?

▸ Have you asked anyone for support since you read this chapter? What happened?

▸ Have you practiced acknowledging anyone since you read this chapter? What happened?

▸ What did you see when you did the Exercises for this chapter?

Discussion Questions for Chapter 13

▸ What do you want to "grow" within yourself, using the Soul of Selling?

▸ What do you want for yourself, and for your selling, as a result of using the Soul of Selling?

▸ Who is the person you've always wanted to be?

Your Soul of Selling Synergy Group can make selling more fun, and also bring you exponential results. In the group itself, you are practicing the principles of seeing the best in everyone, serving others, sharing your vision, being present to your own and others' mental chatter without buying into it and going forward toward your dreams. And others are doing those same things for and with you. Together, you produce a contribution to life and to your own success that is greater than the sum of its parts. Enjoy!